Cold Anger

COLD ANGER

A Story of Faith and Power Politics

by

Mary Beth Rogers

Introduction by Bill Moyers

University of North Texas Press

Requests for permission to reproduce material from this work
should be sent to
Permissions, University of North Texas Press
P. O. Box 13856
Denton, Texas 76203-3856

10 9 8 7 6 5 4 3

The paper used in this book meets the minimum requirements of the
American National Standard for Permanence of Paper for Printed
Library Materials, Z39.48.1984.

**Library of Congress
Cataloging-in-Publication Data**

Rogers, Mary Beth.
    Cold anger : a story of faith and power politics / by
Mary Beth Rogers.
        p.   cm.
    Includes bibliographical references.
    ISBN 0-929398-13-0 : $14.95
    1. Hispanic Americans–Texas–Politics and government. 2.
Cortes, Ernesto. 3. Community organization–Texas. $. Texas–Politics
and government–1951- 5. Hispanic Americans–Politics and government.
6. Community organization–United Sttates.   I. Title.
F395.S75R64   1990
323.1'1680765–dc20   90-35619
                                                           CIP

Table of Contents

Introduction

As Mary Beth Rogers reminds us, when the magazine *Texas Business* published a list of the most powerful Texans a couple of years ago, it included H. Ross Perot and T. Boone Pickens, U.S. Senator Lloyd Bentsen, and the then–Mayor of San Antonio, Henry Cisneros. It also listed Ernesto Cortes.

Ernesto Cortes?

Wait a minute. The man has no money and holds no public office. As Texans usually measure power, Ernie Cortes would be found wanting. He lives simply, talks softly, prays quietly, and is about as charismatic as a load of watermelons. Moreover, he spends altogether too much time in the company of poor people. As there are 32 million such folk in America, Ernie Cortes has little time for the television talk shows that swoon over celebrities, those bright, shining exemplars of contemporary American success. Richard Nixon gets more television exposure during his annual resurrections than 32 million poor people get in a decade. Ernie Cortes has not pitched his tent in the media spotlight.

So what is he doing on the list of most powerful Texans, this vagabond among the powerless? He is there because he empowers others. Ernie's secret weapon is his conviction that power is not something one gathers for personal aggrandizement; it is what you teach others to get for themselves.

Furthermore, he has known for a long time that if absolute power corrupts absolutely (actually, a little will do just as well these days), so does absolute powerlessness. It breeds those twin polluters of the soul, helplessness and hopelessness. And it transforms the processes of democracy from government "of, by, and for the people" into a power grab by lawyers, lobbyists, and legislators (aided and abetted by a media that manufacture frivolous distractions which overwhelm folk who might otherwise notice that their country is being plundered.)

Ernie Cortes abhors the powerlessness of the wounded. He has seen it turn proud people into submissive instruments of alien wills. Growing up, he began to notice how many of his neighbors spent their lives deferring to authority, never questioning, always taking what was done to them as if a rigged lottery were the order of things. "Latinos never developed an understanding of power," he says. "They've been institutionally trained to be passive. Power is nothing more than the ability to act in your behalf. In Spanish, we call the word *poder,* to have capacity, to be able. Real power comes when people have permission to ask questions."

Yes, but permission is rarely granted voluntarily. It has to be wrested from the powers-that-be. And that is what Ernie Cortes tries to help people understand how to do. Here is the second source of his standing: He organizes. More precisely, he trains organizers, and they in turn teach others. You may remember that group of housewives, priests, nuns, and workers at the local Air Force base in San Antonio. What a moment it was when, having been prepared by Ernie Cortes and like-minded allies, they took up their own cause against a callused power structure—and won. "Ordinary" people became experts on rezoning, development, and water and sewer systems. They got action on issues that affected them most immediately. "If we fret about the deficit, we feel paralyzed," says Ernie Cortes. "But we can figure out and strategize and organize to change a neighborhood, get a street paved, improve a school." He likes to quote one of his mentors, the late Saul Alinsky: "Never do for people what they can do for themselves."

So it was that when Ernie first surveyed the Mexican-American community in San Antonio, he found that people were alarmed about the flash floods that threatened their children's lives and their property, not to mention their potable water. This gave his people their mandate. Today, riding around these districts in San Antonio with one of the women who became a leader in the movement, you are regularly invited to behold and admire the water drainage ditches that were built because people organized. You will also be shown other functioning monuments to people power—paved streets and sidewalks, new housing, an access to the freeway.

This power is more than mere muscle. It resonates with a spirituality we last experienced at the height of the civil rights movement in the '60s. Once the San Antonio housewives began to study the law and the rules and began to confront local officials, they often discovered that they knew more than the authorities. This did wonders for their self-esteem and confidence, but it is only in part psychological. Its religious ground is the realization that if I am indeed one of God's children, I must lay claim to my inheritance. If God is my creator, the least I can do is live up to my heritage. Not surprisingly, churches provide Ernie Cortes with a network of kindred souls: pastors, priests, nuns, preachers, and laity who stand, as he tells them, in the tradition of the most effective organizers in history—Moses and Paul.

Ernie Cortes is both conservative and radical. He knows his Bible and his *New York Review of Books*, *The Economist*, *Dissent*, and *World Press Review*. He carries on a running conversation with John Dewey, Albert North Whitehead, Dostoyevski, Herman Melville, and Mark Twain. They have been tutors to a man who considers life a continuing course in adult education, and he borrows from them liberally. Ernie Cortes lives such ideas and tests them against reality; rhetoric is not enough.

I have rarely met a man to whom family and faith mean more, or who better understands the indispensable role of institutions in a fragile society. An obsession with individual rights, he will argue, can weaken the already tenuous ties that hold America's disparate peoples together. Each of us is uniquely an individual, but being alone and isolated is not our natural destiny. Society is dangerously atomized, he warns, and to heal the alienation we must involve individuals not in huge mass organizations but in smaller ones that contribute to the public discourse. He is critical of government programs that foster dependencies while neglecting the innate political capacities of poorer communities. And his summons to citizenship is like a trumpet. What Hannah Arendt called "the joy of public happiness" is in Ernie Cortes contagious. The public square belongs to everyone, he says; fill it!

When I first heard of him many years ago, he was considered a "barrio revolutionary." He helped to organize a boycott of farm products, so arousing the wrath of the wealthy growers that Governor John Connally sent in the Texas Rangers to break up the boycott. Some journalists who saw him then remember Ernie Cortes as a very angry and passionate young man. The anger is no longer visible, but the passion gloriously is. Ernie Cortes still believes that we are created equal—brown, black, and white; that people are citizens before they are consumers; that our future can be what we imagine. He once said of his organizers: "We're a group of people who care about the future because the future is not something abstract. The future is our children, and what happens to them is important." In a society whose political leaders have been willing to wreck the future for the profligacy of the moment, where only the present tense is heard and all that matters is getting it today, and where legitimacy is only conferred in prime time between commercials extolling gratification now, the future is a radical notion. Just as radical is the belief that the poor do not have to accept passively a future created for them by others. To Cortes and company, "power is such a good thing, everyone should have some."

Once-upon-a-time this was a very American idea. Of late it has fallen on hard times, withered beneath an avalanche of manufactured images, public fictions, and the growing domination of stateless corporations. I am indebted—as no doubt you shall be upon reading this robust story of faith and power politics—to Mary Beth Rogers for a wonderful reminder that the American Revolution is not over. It lives on in the cold anger and warm heart of Ernesto Cortes.

More power to him!

—Bill Moyers

Dedicated to the memory of
John Bonner Rogers
1934–1987

Prologue

Cold Anger is a story about a new kind of intervention in politics by working poor people who incorporate their religious values into a struggle for power and visibility. It is about women and men—like Ernesto Cortes, Jr.—who promote public and private hope, political and personal responsibility, community and individual transformation. Even joy. As such, it is a rare story in American politics these days.

Almost unnoticed, growing numbers of working poor people—Hispanics, blacks, whites, Protestants and Catholics, ministers, priests and nuns, shopkeepers, truck drivers, clerks and housewives—are entering politics at the community level in dozens of major cities in Texas and across the nation. They are unusual because they view politics as a *long-term* process to build relationships, new institutions, and humane communities. They are sparked by people like Ernesto Cortes, Jr., community organizer extraordinaire. Cortes is a man of both ideas and action who seeks long-term political change—not just a quick fix. He is engaged in the empowerment of people at a neighborhood and parish level that allows them to exert both personal and political control over their lives. Cortes and his groups have become successful enough to transform the politics of the ninth largest city in the nation and to determine the fate of specific issues in a dozen others, as well as in the entire state of Texas. Because of these successes and the way these groups operate, Ernesto Cortes and the people who participate in the million-member Industrial Areas Foundation network of community organizations in Texas and elsewhere in the nation have the potential to shape a new American grass-roots politics for the 1990s—one that is nurturing to its participants and enriching for our political, religious, and social institutions. More importantly, the local Industrial Areas Foundation groups are virtually the *only* organizations in America that are enticing working poor people to participate in politics.

When I began to see what was happening, I wanted to know why and how, who and what, when and where. So I pursued the story. Then something unexpected happened. Without realizing it initially, I discovered that I had also embarked on a personal voyage that led to the discovery of new emotions and a new view of politics myself. I guess it was only natural, because coinciding with this pursuit were several currents in my own life, much like strong undertows, that pulled me deeper into the stories of these men and women who rejected special-interest and celebrity-based politics in favor of values they considered enduring and eternal.

When I began interviewing Ernesto Cortes, I had already started to reassess my lifetime in politics, which had been my passion since my father sneaked me and my younger sister past security guards into a Democratic party state convention in Dallas in the late 1950s so that we could watch the Democrats tear each other apart—both a participatory and spectator sport in those days of one-party Southern politics. But I loved what I saw at the convention: the fiery speeches, the furious arm-waving, the hot hall, the noise and intrigue, the confrontation between "good and evil." It was a spectacle, a contest, and an adventure. I was intrigued. I wanted more. Politics began to draw me like a magnet, and I was caught in its force field from then on.

As a teenager I stuffed envelopes for candidates and collected "Dollars for Democrats" in dusty parking lots on the State Fair grounds. As a young wife and mother, I forfeited fresh vegetables, plucked eyebrows, and living potted plants to put up campaign signs, plan precinct meetings, or sell the cheap tickets to political fundraisers. I pulled my children away from Saturday morning cartoons to sit in on "big talk" strategy meetings with aspiring candidates or officeholders. I kept card files and voter lists on my dining room table, hosted political receptions in my backyard, registered voters in meat-packing plants, and stayed awake all night every election night until the last votes were counted. I cared passionately about political ideas and issues and believed that what I was doing would have an impact on people's lives. Politics for me was both a compulsion and a joy. It was a necessity!

But by the 1980s, there were disturbances in the magnetic field of politics. I was growing weary. And I was increasingly bothered by the shift I had been witnessing over the years from volunteer to professional politics—even though I personally had benefited from the shift. I had been married since I was barely 20 years old to John Rogers, a journalist who turned himself into a master technician and political strategist for progressive and labor causes. He was a campaign professional, a political expert. I, too, had been paid for my services in political campaigns and had moved in and out of local and state government at increasingly higher levels. Together, John and I had been on the inside of Texas politics for a number of years. *Texas Monthly* magazine once called us one of Texas' most powerful political couples. I had even conducted workshops across the country under the auspices of the old National Women's Education Fund to teach women how to run for office and win, using the latest in the new campaign technology.

Yet I was growing cynical about the transformation of electoral politics and the almost shamlike manufacture of voter consent that gives the appearance of democracy but delivers less and less of its substance. Both inside government and outside, in the process of capturing the machinery of government, we were moving to a system dominated by "experts." Ordinary people increasingly were left out. But the essence of democracy is the concept of popular control and direct participation by people themselves in the decisions that affect them. We were moving away from bedrock democratic values built around the role of the "citizen" decision-maker. Also, I was seeing fewer young idealists caught by the politics magnet that had snared me 30 years earlier. That worried me, too. But what was really beginning to weigh on me was that so many candidates and officeholders, some of whom I now knew well, seemed to look and sound alike, with images and words carefully crafted by campaign operatives who, I felt, relied on a too-simplistic reading of polling data from which they fabricated superficial themes—themes that appeared to speak to voter concerns but that rarely touched fundamental truths.

Political consultants multiplied faster than jack rabbits, increasing exponentially from one campaign season to the next. Activities previously handled by volunteers were taken over by experts in direct mail, telephone canvassing, cluster polling, message development, image managing, media buying, television production, speech coaching, and on and on. The times and technology demanded it—if you wanted to win.

Of course, you had to have money to operate in this arena, which meant that unless you had personal wealth, you had to raise money constantly. To be successful at the money game, you tailored your views and votes to those who had the money, or you kept your mouth shut on issues and ideas of controversy. As a result, most politicians said essentially the same thing, with a few chosen code words beeped out to signal an affinity with certain special-interest groups. But for most voters, the differences between politicians were arrayed in shadings of gray, rarely coming close to any substantive hue on the political color spectrum. With one politician virtually indistinguishable from another, voters simply stopped voting. What good did it do? No one seemed to care anymore. And I was not sure I did either. Besides, there were other disturbances in my life beginning to break up the magnetic field of politics and lessen its pull.

One was John Rogers' cancer diagnosis in mid-1983 when he was in his professional prime. John's illness forced us to examine our lives in a way we had not since we married more than 20 years earlier. We particularly focused on family and our children, and what we wanted to make of the time we had left—together and separately. With this kind of reflection came a renewed desire by both of us to recapture some of our early political idealism, now frayed by the years of experience. It hit us during one of the most difficult times of his treatment when John told a physician at M.D. Anderson Cancer Treatment

Center in Houston that seeing the poor treated as royally as the rich in that great publicly funded hospital reminded him of why he had gotten into politics in the first place. "I was a liberal who believed in people," he said. "But then I got caught up in the fun of it all, and I became a technician instead."

Our new idealism embarrassed us. For the most part, we kept it to ourselves.

All of this was weighing on my mind when Texas Treasurer Ann Richards and I were in Washington on a snowy evening in February 1984. Ann had been my longtime friend and colleague in a number of causes—a few raucous campaigns to elect both good women and men to public office. Most recently, we had collaborated on a major museum exhibition about the history of women in Texas. When she was elected treasurer, Ann asked me to become her chief deputy, and we had the distinction in 1983 of becoming the first women in modern Texas government to occupy the top two positions in a state agency. Now we were in Washington calling on officials of the Federal Reserve Board, and through the efforts of our friend Carlton Carl, we had the good fortune to have dinner one night with some of our favorite members of the Texas congressional delegation—U.S. Representatives John Bryant of Dallas and Ron Coleman and his wife Debbie from El Paso. Fiery Texas Agriculture Commissioner Jim Hightower was also in town, and he joined us too.

Going out on a snowy night is always a memorable event for Texans, but the muffling of Washington sounds and sights by that white blanket also made me reflective—and surprisingly more talkative than usual. The weather gave us the restaurant to ourselves and I was seated next to Congressman Bryant, apple-cheeked, serious, and apparently as reflective as I. Before coming to Congress, Bryant was the major strategist for a reform claque of legislators who served in the Texas House in the 1970s. He was a straight arrow—ethical, smart, and conscientious about public service—and the only politician I knew who blushed when he got a compliment. His congressional district in east Dallas was a mix of blue-collar workers, blacks, middle-class business owners, and professionals, and Bryant had worked with my husband on a number of issues over the years. Although we knew each other, I did not know much about Bryant's background. We began talking about the things that drew us to politics.

"For me," I began cautiously, "it was both the excitement of the game and the teachings of the Methodist church." Pause. Did I really say that? Should I continue? In my political circles, you always handled a discussion of religion and politics cautiously because in the Bible Belt, anyone who mixed religion and politics was either a scoundrel, a soft touch, or a fool. If you were from the progressive wing of the state party, as were most of the people at our table that evening, you wouldn't hobnob with any of them. But I caught a glint in Bryant's eye.

"You too?" he asked, smiling.

Encouraged, I continued. "I believed all that stuff about 'loving your neighbor,' 'blessed are the poor,' taking care of the 'least of these,'" I said.

We laughed. Then Bryant revealed that his earliest political impulses stemmed from the same Methodist teachings. Both of us were somewhat embarrassed. He was a member of Congress. I was a back-room operative. Some people might even think we were political sophisticates! Yet we had just admitted to each other that we had been drawn to politics, at least in part, because we believed what we had learned in the Methodist Youth Fellowship! Both of us had obviously imbibed the same tenets of the old Social Gospel, which had penetrated Methodist and other Protestant churches after the turn of the century. Its premise was that, if you believed in the Gospel, you had a responsibility to correct social and economic wrongs and to work for a just society. The beliefs underlying the Social Gospel were those that had propelled so many Protestant ministers into the civil rights movement, the antiwar efforts, and the urban poverty wars. Although I had long since left the Methodist church, its Social Gospel seeds had been planted in me at the little Greenland Hills Methodist neighborhood church in Dallas. And those same seeds had been sown in Congressman Bryant's neighborhood church, as well. Politics became for each of us the logical field in which to harvest them.

That conversation stayed with me. A few months later, I was at Scholz's Beer Garden in Austin with friends when I met Bill Shearer, a compelling and literate conversationalist who owned a small regional publishing firm and who had struggled to outgrow the fundamentalist beliefs of his Nazarene preacher father. Our talk that evening turned to the mix of religion and politics, often a poisonous stew that endangers democracy. But when I told Shearer about my conversation with Congressman Bryant, he thought it would be interesting to develop a book about successful "moderate" political players in the 1980s whose initial motivations to enter politics derived from basic religious values. The point of the book would be to see if genuine religious sentiment could be injected into the political arena without launching the narrow, extremist theocracy that fundamentalists such as Jerry Falwell seemed to propose. Shearer encouraged me to pursue the idea, and we came up with a list of people I would interview. Along with Bryant, Ernesto Cortes, Jr. was on the list.

I had known Cortes more than 20 years earlier in San Antonio when he was a young activist involved with the United Farm Workers and I was a housewife with two babies helping conduct voter registration and get-out-the-vote drives on San Antonio's Hispanic West Side. Since the early 1960s, San Antonio had changed enormously, and many people considered Ernesto Cortes largely responsible. He organized one of the grandest and most long-lasting political coups in the nation by turning San Antonio's once-closed, Anglo-dominated city government into an open community that elected Henry Cisneros its first Hispanic mayor in 1981. The vehicle for this shift in power was a Mexican-American–based and Catholic church–based organization called Communities Organized for Public Service, or COPS. Although Cortes consistently maintained a low profile, politicians were becoming increasingly aware of him because COPS-like organizations were springing up in cities throughout Texas, New York, California, and other states.

I was very interested in the Catholic church connection to this successful political organizing, and Cortes was kind enough to give me unlimited access to him and his organizations for the book I planned to write. But after following Cortes around for several months, I realized I was seeing something different in politics. I was seeing more than the story of the religious or political motivations of one man, or even San Antonio's transformation through a new brand of church-based social activism. I was, instead, witness to a new kind of faith and power politics—gritty, realistic, and successful. Unfolding in front of me was the story of more than 400,000 men and women who made up the network of Industrial Areas Foundation organizations in Texas, and how they were developing themselves to assume power and to act responsibly once they got it.

Since I had been in politics, I had never seen anything that seemed to reach people so deeply and wrench from them such a commitment to make "unimportant" people important in the public life of their communities. Cortes seemed to be building new political institutions and developing a new kind of political participant. And his organizations and people were connected not only with the Catholic church, but with mainline Protestant denominations as well. The political intervention of these church people seemed to be creating intelligent political discussion on behalf of poor families and neighborhoods, providing a stark contrast to fundamentalist involvement in single-issue, all-or-nothing conservative politics. What Cortes was doing was also more interesting to me because it seemed to transform individual lives and give ordinary people a sense of personal power that allowed them to operate as equals with the "experts" in corporate board rooms, city halls, and in the state capital. As a result, I decided to focus on Ernesto Cortes' new kind of religious-based politics in Texas, and this book began to take shape.

Most of my research and more than half of my manuscript was completed by late 1987, when John Rogers suddenly died—having survived his cancer and its debilitating treatment only to succumb to his old childhood nemesis, asthma. It was 1989 before I got back into the book, and new emotions and new insights led me to throw away everything I had written before and to start all over from scratch. Somehow, my basic political cynicism no longer provided an adequate framework with which to view either politics or religion, or to deal adequately with what Cortes was doing. And that led me to understand one additional current in my life, one that grew stronger as I emerged from the undertow of grief: the renewal of my own political hope.

Ernesto Cortes and the Industrial Areas Foundation were bringing people back into politics. They were attracting men and women whose values were based on the belief in the fundamental worth of the individual and the understanding that only within the framework of a caring human "community" could the individual grow, develop, and rise to his or her potential. What's more, these were people who had an appreciation for the value of give-and-take and genuine public discourse. They believed in the joy of politics and in its inherent worth as a way to participate in the world. They believed in the excitement and vitality of practicing "citizenship," giving it an expanded meaning beyond what is usually encapsulated in civics textbooks. To Cortes and the people he was bringing to the political process, a "citizen" is someone who matters, someone who becomes visible—and thus worthy—by taking action to benefit the common good. A citizen is someone who can operate effectively, personally and politically, because he or she understands the uses and misuses of power—and its sources. In many ways, the people Cortes was bringing into politics were more sophisticated than the "experts" who were running politics and managing the politicians. And they came closer to grasping the inherent wisdom that underlies our democracy: that government should not be a distinction between us and them—the experts and the ignorant, the governing and the governed. It should be "we, the people"—not them, the government.

For me, then, the significance of this story is how Ernesto Cortes, Jr. and other leaders of the Industrial Areas Foundation organizations are helping ordinary men and women awaken to their power to become "we, the people." It is a story that makes me feel hopeful once again about American politics. And it is a story that revealed to me the depth of underlying anger felt by men and women for whom the idea of becoming "we, the people" is so distant.

Anger? Yes, anger. Which, for the working poor, arises most often from being ignored, invisible, left out, overlooked, dismissed, and burdened by the small frustrations and daily humiliations of a constant struggle to get by. But the anger I saw among the working-class and poor families Cortes represents is not one based on sour resentments or a false sense of entitlement. Rather, it is an anger that seethes at the injustices of life and transforms itself into a compassion for those hurt by life. It is an anger rooted in direct experience and held in collective memory. It is the kind of anger that can energize a democracy—because it can lead to the first step in changing politics.

Ernesto Cortes, Jr. and the people of the Industrial Areas Foundation organizations have chosen to be energized personally and politically by their anger. In turn, they are changing the political process wherever they participate. That is because anger for Cortes and the people he organizes is an emotion of hope—not of despair. Ernesto Cortes is helping new political participants take the hot impulse of their anger and cool it down so that it can become a useful tool to improve individual lives and the quality of the common community. For them, "cold anger" reflects the hope of change.

Our history reveals that Americans have been trying to expand the concept of "we, the people" for more than 200 years. Sometimes we have succeeded, sometimes we have failed. But the process has always challenged our most thoughtful citizens. Ernesto Cortes teaches that it is the process of becoming "we, the people" that is important in itself. And, by focusing on the "becoming," Cortes and the new political leaders of the Industrial Areas Foundation are revitalizing not only themselves, but our continuing American experiment in democracy as well. I believe they offer hope for the survival and reality of "we, the people."

Several individuals provided valuable advice that helped me develop this story. They are Anne Blocker, Dr. Betty Sue Flowers, Geoff Rips, Ellen Temple, and Fran Vick. I am grateful to them and to my children, Billy Rogers and Eleanor Rogers Lee, who encouraged me to continue the story when I put it aside. I am particularly indebted to Ernesto and Oralia Cortes and to the men and women of the Industrial Areas Foundation who gave their time and shared their lives with me.

Part One

*The leader's fundamental act is to
induce people to be aware or conscious
of what they feel—to feel their true
needs so strongly, to define their values
so meaningfully, that they can be
moved to purposeful action.*

James MacGregor Burns
Leadership

1

Moses and Paul:
The World's Greatest Organizers

Dallas, 1986

"Anybody remember Moses?" Ernesto Cortes Jr. asks a group of farmers and farm activists from 40 states who have come to Dallas to discuss their problems and hear Cortes speak at a Farm Crisis Workers Conference.[1] A few members of the audience nod and look at each other as if to say, "Who the hell is this and what have we gotten ourselves into?"

Cortes is the coordinator of a dozen or so Industrial Areas Foundation (IAF) organizations in Texas, such as San Antonio's COPS and the Rio Grande Valley Interfaith. Because of his 20-year community organizing career in Texas and around the nation, Cortes has become a legend among American political activists and a source on Hispanic politics for journalists from the *New York Times,* the *Wall Street Journal,* and a slew of other publications. The prestigious MacArthur Foundation gave him one of its "genius" grants and $204,000 to do with as he saw fit. *Esquire* identified him as one of the people who represented America "at its best."[2] *Texas Business* magazine called Cortes one of the most powerful people in Texas—along with Ross Perot and corporate raider extraordinaire T. Boone Pickens.[3] Somehow, with all of this, you don't expect him to be talking about Moses.

"The two greatest organizers historically were Moses and

Paul," Cortes begins his remarks to the farmers. "Both men knew how to build networks and build broad-based organizations. Both understood the politics of organization. But Moses had a crisis on his hands when he brought the chosen people out of Egypt and they spent all those years just wandering around in the desert. He's got all these folks coming at him saying, 'You know, things were a lot better in Egypt. We had a lot of good times—what are you offering us here? Nothing but crummy food. We want some chitlins . . . we want some tamales . . .'"[4]

People in the audience begin to laugh. Obviously, this is to be no ordinary Bible lesson. Cortes also loosens up. With eyes shining like black marbles, he becomes almost impish as he paces in front of the group in his ambling professorial manner. His smile breaks the heavy spell cast by his weighty bulk and bearing; he looks like a freight train about to sprout wings and leave the fast track for more fanciful ventures. He leans into the crowd.

"So what's Moses' reaction to this crisis?" he asks as he peers over his glasses and waits a moment before answering his own question. "Well, old Moses says, 'It's too heavy for me, but it's *my* burden. It's *my* problem.'"

Cortes waits for the farmers to work through this thought with him, to participate in the moment. "Why is it his burden and why is it his problem?" he asks.

But the audience is still unsure what Cortes expects of them, and they are silent. So Cortes answers his own question again. "Because he's allowed people to dump all of their problems on him. Everybody comes to Moses and says, 'Okay, now you solve it, Moses. Listen, you're our big leader, you're our big organizer, you're the guy who led us out, you've got the business, you've got all this relationship with Yahweh, so you're the guy who's got to solve this particular problem. You've solved every other problem."

Cortes again tries to entice his audience to respond. "But what else is going on here?"

"They were all lazy," a farmer finally responds.

Someone else shouts, "They were depending on Moses more than they should have done and they should have been depending more on themselves."

Cortes almost leaps at the response, "Yeah! that's right!" With excitement in his voice, he begins to enunciate his words very slowly and deliberately. "You see, there's an Iron Rule in organizing. It is a little different from the Golden Rule. The Iron Rule says: *Never, ever, do for people what they can do for themselves.* And it's a very difficult rule to follow. Moses had been historically violating the Iron Rule. He was doing *for* people. He was solving their problems. He was servicing and maintaining them. He was meeting their every need. He was doing all their thinking for them." Cortes pauses and looks around to make sure the farmers are still with him.

"When people have a charismatic leader who does all their thinking, they become dependent," Cortes says. "They become passive. They lack initiative. Their anger turns in on themselves and it's no use to them. So in this situation what did God say to Moses?"

"You haven't got a choice," an audience member shouts.

"Well, he didn't say just that, but you're perceptive anyway. No, the Lord said unto Moses," Cortes reads from a Bible he had placed on the table beside him, "'Gather unto me seventy men who thou knowest to be the elders of the people . . . and I will come down and . . . take of the spirit which is upon thee and will put it on them; and they shall bear the burden of the people with thee, that thou shall not bear it by thyself alone.'"[5]

"Now what did old Moses say to this?" Cortes asks. "Did he say 'Great idea God, you got it.' Right? No. He resists, like we would do. But this time the Lord gets a little angry. He says, 'Moses, you're a jerk.'"

"Did God say that?" someone shouts amid crowd laughter.

"Well, no. That's just my exegesis of what he said," Cortes laughs with the crowd. "But Moses finally obeys, and the Lord 'took of the spirit and gave it to the seventy.' And they go off and organize a hunting party for quail or something and Moses doesn't have to do all the work. Now, the times were not unique, the people were not unique. They were just like you and me. So what's the point of the story for us today in the United States?"

"We need to organize a hunting party?" an audience member responds.

"Well maybe . . . but you farmers have a crisis—*I* don't have a crisis—*you've* got a crisis. Go back and read the Bible, read about how Moses felt, with the world on his shoulders, losing his sense of humor, not seeing that this crisis was an opportunity to test out his organizations, to develop leadership. The Chinese symbol for crisis is what? Danger and opportunity. We can see this crisis as an opportunity to do some strategic planning or thinking and ask some fundamental questions about the nature of the real crisis."

Then, Cortes becomes more deliberate. The freight train returns to the fast track of his destination. "For me, the crisis is a misunderstanding of power, a naiveté about power and a total unwillingness of people to appreciate the importance of politics. Politics, not in the electoral sense, not in the sense of electing men and women to public office, not the kind of politics that we have in this country which is not really politics. Every four years we have an electronic plebiscite, which does not have anything at all to do with politics."

The audience is rapt. Cortes continues, his tone more serious, his voice dropping in range. "Aristotle sees politics as discussion and decision-making about family, about property, and about education. Aristotle talks about politics as public discourse which enables and ennobles a spirit because it allows you to cross the boundary between public and private and move beyond self-centeredness into relationship with other people and engage them and bargain with them, fight and ultimately compromise with them. That's politics. What we have every four years are these plebiscites which are about media, ad men, marketing techniques, pollsters. So we've totally trivialized our politics, made them superficial and somewhat distorted and deformed. As a result, people are in revolt against politics. They think all politicians are phonies. They think of all politicians as lacking in substance. They see politicians as being self-centered and egotistical. And unfortunately, in eight out of 10 cases they're right.

"Well, I'd like to suggest that the real opportunity that comes out of this crisis is for us to begin now to develop an appreciation for what real politics offers. Real politics offers an opportunity to engage people at the core of their values, their vision, their imagination. It begins to offer them some possibilities for change, for transformation of self and of community by beginning to deal with some fundamental issues which affect families.

"Real politics requires understanding of some other values, values like pluralism, compromise, discourse, quid pro quo, and most importantly, relationships—how you begin to build relationships.

"Organizing is a fancy word for relationship building. No organizer ever organizes a community. What an organizer does is identify, test out, and develop leadership. And the leadership builds the relationships and the networks and following that does the organizing.

"If I want to organize you, I don't sell you an idea. What I do, if I'm smart, is try to find out what's your interest. What are your dreams? I try to kindle your imagination, stir the possibilities, and then propose some ways in which you can act on those dreams and act on those values and act on your own visions. You've got to be the owner. Otherwise, it's my cause, my organization. You've got nothing!"

2

We Are Willing to Sacrifice

La Meza, 1988

Five hundred miles south of Dallas is La Meza, Texas. A desolate little stop on a back road, La Meza is a Rio Grande Valley *colonia,* a neighborhood of 65 Hispanic families, perhaps 400 people in all. It is just outside of Mercedes, which has a population of 12,000 in the county of Hidalgo at the southern tip of Texas where the Rio Grande flows into the Gulf of Mexico. Here, the world seems to dwindle. Even the low, wide horizon, the orange groves, and the patchwork fields of onions, cabbage, or carrots cannot stop the feeling that you are in a land that shrinks its people, forcing them inward, isolating them from their nearest neighbors, from the rest of America, and perhaps even from themselves.

La Meza is directly across the road from the Sunrise Hill Park, a public park with picnic tables, playground equipment, and a sweeping sprinkler system to keep the grass a bright winter green. But unlike the park, La Meza's people, mostly migrant farmworkers, have no green grass. They have no water. Or sewers. Or paved streets. To drink, they must take a water jug to the Sunset Drive-In Grocery where the paved road by the park begins. At the grocery store, they pay the owner 25 cents to use an ordinary outdoor spigot to fill their water jugs. To wash their clothes or dishes or faces, they cannot afford the tap water and so they fill their barrels from pools of water in the irrigation drainage ditches that hold the runoff from nearby vegetable fields. The ditches are full of pesticides and herbicides, and the people of La Meza know that water in the ditches is bad for them, but what else can they do? Water is water. And, sometimes, life itself.

Elida Bocanegra and 20 La Meza residents meet the van pulling into the parking lot of the Sunset Drive-In Grocery. Young couples with sniffling children are waiting. One woman holds a little girl of about 2 whose left eye is encrusted with a blackened tumor the size of a lemon. Several older men and women are in the crowd, the men in work clothes standing back and a little apart from the group, their wrinkles and calluses granting them rights to a certain skepticism that they wear on their faces like translucent masks. A boy of 6 holds a small sign, its message hand-lettered in red paint: "Help us Ann Richards. We need water to drink."

On this warm day in February, Texas Treasurer Ann Richards and a small group of state officials come to La Meza on a "fact-finding" mission.[1] Richards, the witty and attractive grandmother who had made her mark both in Texas and nationally, had been invited to tour the *colonias* by Valley Interfaith, a coalition of 40 Rio Grande Valley churches representing about 55,000 people who were waging a campaign to call national attention to the plight of people in the *colonias*. Perhaps Richards' ties to the financial networks in Texas and New York could help. But first, she wanted the facts.

Statistically, the four counties of the Rio Grande Valley contain the poorest people in the United States—the highest unemployment and the lowest per capita income in the nation.[2] Almost 100,000 people live in the Valley *colonias*, the 400-plus unincorporated rural communities unique to the 900-mile Texas-Mexican border. *Colonia* is a Spanish word for neighborhood, and along the Texas border, the *colonias* have come to signify a particular kind of rural slum with conditions more akin to Nicaragua or Honduras than the United States of America.

More facts: open sewer ditches, unpaved streets, no running water, and in some cases, no electricity. Clapboard houses often have dirt floors and wall-to-wall beds for growing families. Children have chronic dysentery, skin rashes, lice, and hepatitis; dark yellow stains mark their teeth from the chemical-laden drinking water. The Valley has the highest incidence of parasitic intestinal diseases outside of the Third World. Shallow water wells are frequently polluted by overflowing septic tanks. After heavy rains, people in the *colonias* literally drink their own sewage. It is a public health nightmare. But because fly-by-night developers established these unregulated subdivisions in rural areas outside of any Texas governmental jurisdiction, the water and sewer problems are suspended in a bureaucratic swamp that most politicians hesitate to enter.

Mrs. Bocanegra, 60ish, small, and serious in her turquoise cotton pants suit, calls the group together, makes polite introductions, and tells the state officials about the problems of La Meza. She has the facts they want. There is a water main along the county road a few hundred yards from the homes of La Meza. She has the figures they need. It would take only $29,000 to extend a line from the main water pipe to provide hookups for the residents of La Meza. She has questions. "How is it possible to go without water in the richest nation in the world?" she asks.

Mrs. Bocanegra's words are echoed by old Father José Mateus, whose mismatched clothes, scuffed shoes, and kindly smile indicate that he might be a true Christian of the Roman and Rio Grande Valley Catholic church. The church was joining with Valley Interfaith in this quest for water and good sense. A powerful endorsement. But whereas it may have been Father Mateus and the Catholic church that supported her, it was Ernesto Cortes and Valley Interfaith that had given Mrs. Bocanegra and the residents of La Meza the tools to act. Tools that allow Mrs. Bocanegra to confront the officials before her. She does not shrink from the encounter. In fact, Mrs. Bocanegra seems to expand as she speaks. Her voice gains strength. Her shoulders rise and arch with her composure. Her black eyes fix on the group with determination. She is like a fourth-grade teacher patiently explaining the logic of the multiplication tables. It is simply illogical for the people of La Meza to have no water.

"We are willing to pay whatever we can," Mrs. Bocanegra says. "We are willing to sacrifice, if we just have the chance."

The group listens to Mrs. Bocanegra. They ask questions.

They look at the spigot, the houses, the road. They commiserate with the residents. They shake hands, and they leave.

In the old days in Texas, a trip like this would soon be forgotten; after all, what could you do with such bureaucracy, such poverty! But the state officials cannot forget. For one thing, their hearts are touched, and their consciences pricked. For another, Valley Interfaith was developed by the Industrial Areas Foundation, and its organizations in Texas are not to be trifled with. The Valley Interfaith invitation to see and help the *colonias* is not extended or accepted casually. When Valley Interfaith issues an invitation like this and when a politician accepts it, it means that each agrees to be held accountable for both words and deeds, to strip away the public show that often passes for politics, and to get down to public business. Which, in this case, is to find a way to deal with the public health needs of thousands of Texans in the Rio Grande Valley. Ann Richards is a wise enough politician to understand the unwritten contract.

"I'm not going to promise you anything I can't deliver," she tells the La Meza residents. "But I will stand by you and work with you to do what we can *together*."

3

We Need Power
to Protect What We Value

Austin, 1988

Charles "Lefty" Morris and I spot Ernie Cortes walking ahead of us into the Texas French Bread Bakery and Deli. We are going to meet him for a late lunch. Morris is a successful attorney and former president of the Texas Trial Lawyers Association who has recently grown disenchanted with the gritty little skirmishes of political combat and has been seeking ideas about how to change the structure of the war itself. He had heard about Cortes and wanted to know more about him.

Cortes has just come from a doctor's appointment, where he was warned one more time to shed a few pounds. Only about 5 feet 7 inches tall, Cortes' genetic tendency to be overweight worries his wife Oralia, but his obvious comfort with his teddy-bear body belies worry and lends a surprisingly sensual air to him. It is hard not to be drawn to his dark eyes, which compete with a bushy, graying mustache to dominate his face. Physically, he is almost oblivious of himself. His attire is conservative, but he is as mindful of his clothes as a 3-year-old. During the day, his shirttail might work its way out of his trousers, his tie might be witness to his meals, or the unnoticed string of a price tag might dangle from his sleeve. No matter—to him or to anyone else. Cortes clearly does not dress to be the center of attention. In fact, throughout his career, he has tried to deflect the spotlight from himself to the people who hold his organizations together. With each of his successes, however, that has been harder to do.

We order salads and sandwiches, none of us yielding to the whiffs that fill the air of fresh-baked sugar-and-cinnamon concoctions. And we talk. With Cortes, talk is always more compelling than sugar. His conversation is colorful and gossipy, yet informed and infused with ideas. In an hour, his topics can cover the decline of the American manufacturing system, the Liberation Theology, Thomas Jefferson, Paul's letters to the Corinthians, the clumsy infidelities of a well-known public official, and a confession that he once shaved his trademark mustache because his daughter, then 7 years old, would not kiss him until he did. But today, the talk is about his church-based organizing in politics.

"The work we do is about power and about building power and teaching people how to organize around their own interests, how to be effective," Cortes tells Morris.

The "we" Cortes describes is the Industrial Areas Foundation network of church-based organizations that represent at least 400,000 people in Texas. Nationally, they are linked with similar organizations in New York, California, Maryland, New Jersey, and other states, and they reach more than a million people through their affiliations. Cortes serves as the peripatetic manager of the Texas network, as well as its lead fundraiser. He is also one of the five members of the governing cabinet of the IAF, which has developed both the philosophy and organizing techniques underlying Cortes' successes. Successes that mean changes in the lives of ordinary men and women, not necessarily fame or fortune for Cortes.

Although I had known Cortes when I lived in San Antonio in the 1960s, I had only a vague notion that he was behind some of the public school reform efforts in Texas in 1984 and that he played a role in the dramatic political and social transformation that San Antonio had been experiencing since the mid-1970s. Now something new was happening in Texas politics to cause thousands of church people—ministers, priests, nuns, and laypeople—to flood the public arena, operating with the same Bible in hand but with an entirely different social agenda from the religious fundamentalists who were thundering into American politics from the right. Something out-of-the-ordinary was happening when 10,000 Texas church members rallied on the State Capitol steps to demand more state money for poor schools in places like Mercedes, Edgewood, and Socorro—and to pledge themselves to work for the taxes to raise it. Or, when Houston church leaders brought petitions bearing 30,000 signatures to the state Public Utility Commission to stop a local electric rate increase. Or, when 1,800 Rio Grande Valley church members confronted federal Environmental Protection Agency officials over the dumping of PCB-laden toxic wastes in the Gulf of Mexico. Or, when San Antonio's church activists defeated a "Proposition 13"–style city-wide referendum to put a cap on public spending—widely seen as hurting the city's poor residents. Or, when every major statewide elected official in Texas trooped down to the *colonias* and promised to help Valley Interfaith improve conditions there.

Something was happening all right, but not many of us involved in Texas politics knew exactly what it was. And it was not because Ernesto Cortes was secretive or in hiding. It was only that he did not seek the limelight or the company of political party operatives or send out a stream of press releases announcing his victories or intentions. That was simply not his style. When I rediscovered Cortes again in 1985, I came to realize that he was like one of those dark strong stars pushed so far back in the universe that its pulsations are charted and considered with awe long before its presence is fully defined. I and thousands of others were feeling the pulsations put out by Cortes, sensing the depth and mass of his new kind of politics, without knowing exactly what he was doing or why.

But I did recognize change. During the 10 years I lived in San Antonio in the 1960s, someone drowned in a flood almost every time there was a torrential downpour. But that no longer happens because Communities Organized for Public Service, or COPS, under Cortes, got the city to spend more than $500 million for West Side improvements, including storm sewer systems that have virtually ended flooding there. In El Paso, children don't have to drink or bathe in contaminated water because one of the IAF organizations got the city to extend water and sewer hookups to 20,000 people in a *colonia*. Houston has more neighborhood police patrols in the black inner city, and flooding is no longer a problem in some predominantly black neighborhoods. Austin police have cleaned up public housing dope dens. Fort Worth has more school crossing guards and training programs to get parents of poor children involved in the schools. All across Texas, young pregnant women who are poor now get prenatal care in state health clinics because the local IAF groups joined forces at the state level to get legislators to approve a model indigent health-care bill helping 200,000 people. Working poor people convinced millionaire Ross Perot that his plans for education reform would be incomplete in 1984 unless he joined them to get the legislature to pump more than $800 million into poor school districts in yet another attempt to "equalize" the money Texas spent on its schools from one district to another. The Texas Legislature in 1989 authorized a $100 million bond package for sewer and water improvements for the *colonias,* and 60 percent of Texas voters approved the program in a statewide vote.[1] Even Mrs. Bocanegra and the residents of La Meza now have water to drink.[2]

One Texas journal said the presence of the IAF groups had "changed the equations of power at the Capitol."[3] But the real significance of the IAF's accomplishments is that the political dialogue is shifting in Texas. The questions are no longer whether to help the *colonias,* but *how to do it;* not whether to shift state money from rich to poor school districts, but *how to do it;* not whether to provide health care to poor women and children, but *how to do it.* And Cortes and the IAF organizations, which are training a new group of political leaders, like Elida Bocanegra, make it possible for these public discussions to be taken seriously. So seriously, in fact, that when I told my son I was going to write about Ernesto Cortes, Jr., he warned me, "Watch out, Mom. He's a tough sonofabitch."

In 1984, Billy Rogers had seen a Cortes explosion of anger in then–Texas Governor Mark White's office when a top White assistant failed to keep a promise to Cortes. Cortes had been indelicate enough to raise his voice, even cause a scene in the reception room where other visitors waited to see the governor. The tirade terrified the governor's aide. In only a matter of minutes, he had ushered Cortes into an inner office, and Billy Rogers had made an important decision: He would make darn sure he never promised Ernesto Cortes, Jr. anything he could not deliver.

Incidents like this have caused a lot of people to come to the same conclusion. Most savvy Texas politicians respect Cortes. Some even fear him—a fear he acknowledges, even encourages. Yet sometimes he wishes it were not so. "It's unfortunate that fear is the only way to get some politicians to respect your power," Cortes says. "They refuse to give you respect. They don't recognize your dignity. So we have to act in ways to get their attention. We don't always choose fear. In some areas, what we have going for us is the *amount* of fear we can generate. We got where we are because people fear and loathe us. They fear us not just because we turn out votes for them, but for what we can do to them."[4]

This is tough talk. But not idle. Cortes' power comes because his voter registration and get-out-the-vote drives have repeatedly demonstrated election-day clout. He knows—and teaches—nitty-gritty electoral politics, paying attention to precinct analysis, understanding polls and strategic planning, and using telephone banks and door-to-door canvasses. But Cortes also teaches something more basic: that politicians work for the people who elect them. Which means that his organizations respect an officeholder for performance, not for position. Deference is out of the question.

"When you've got somebody working for you, you don't bow and scrape," said a Cortes-trained leader of one of the organizations.[5] So the groups watch, remind, persist, confront, and challenge public officials to respond to public needs. And if officials fail to act, the IAF groups do not hesitate to expose their inattention, insincerity, or incompetence—in public. San Antonio's COPS once slammed then-Mayor Henry Cisneros with a sarcastically critical "A-Ya-Toll-A" award for hobnobbing with foreign dignitaries and ignoring San Antonio's citizens. And Cisneros was one of COPS' closest political allies![6]

The elaborately staged "accountability" sessions of the IAF groups have become notorious. Officeholders are usually seated on a stage in an auditorium facing several hundred, or even thousands, of church people waving banners and revved up for action. One of the group's leaders reads a statement or asks a series of specific questions, and the officials have only about three to five minutes to respond. There is no time for equivocation. A simple "yes" or "no" is about all that is allowed. Many elected officials talk privately about how much they hate the "adversarial nature" of the sessions, which generate an almost paranoiac dread among some politicians—even at the national level. In the 1984 presidential election, Walter Mondale agreed to meet with Valley Interfaith leaders while he was on a campaign swing through South Texas. But he had been so thoroughly forewarned about the organization's confrontational tactics that he pulled one of Valley Interfaith's leaders aside and said, "Just don't do anything to embarrass me in front of the media."[7]

"There are only two ways to build power like this," Cortes tells Morris. "It takes organized money or organized people. We're obviously not going to have a huge concentration of money, so when we're talking about power as a social concept, we're talking about two or more people coming together with a plan and acting on it."

"Well, if you get power," Morris asks, "aren't you going to be corrupted like everyone else?"

"We may be," Cortes admits. "But we're trying to teach a system of internal accountability so that won't happen."

As I listen to Cortes talk about power and accountability, I remember one of the first internal evaluation sessions I saw him conduct for members of the Metropolitan Congregational Alliance (MCA) in San Antonio.[8] It was after a meeting at which about 500 MCA members and other neighborhood representatives had challenged San Antonio's popular Mayor Cisneros to reevaluate the city's growth and annexation policies. Even though Cisneros differed with calls for restraints on new North Side development, he agreed to attend the meeting because he had a long and deep relationship with MCA's sister organization, the West Side COPS, which some political observers believed helped him in 1981 to become the city's first Hispanic mayor in 150 years. But MCA almost lost control of the meeting with Cisneros because the non-MCA members from the neighborhoods cornered the mayor and disrupted the agenda.

An hour before the rally at the Colonial Hills United Meth-

odist Church, neighborhood representatives insisted on changing the meeting agenda, demanding to confront the mayor on
issues that had not been scheduled for discussion. MCA leaders
were appalled, and they threatened to call off the meeting even
as hundreds of people began to arrive. But a last-minute compromise allowed one of the neighborhood leaders to present
her concerns to the mayor, which she did in a long harangue
that forced the mayor to agree to a separate meeting with her
group.

The experience left a residue of frustration among MCA
leaders, and they wanted to talk with Cortes about it. "We lost
control of the action because they were the ones who had the
people there," one leader told Cortes.

"What does that tell you?" Cortes asked.

"We didn't do our homework," someone said. "We didn't
turn out our own people."

"We also totally misread the situation," another MCA leader
said. "We thought the neighborhood associations would follow
our lead."

"I question my own leadership for not knowing how to handle this," one of the meeting organizers added.

Then, Cortes cut off the self-recrimination and shifted to a
more constructive analysis. "Don't be too hard on yourselves,"
he advised. "You made some mistakes, but you averted a disaster. The blunder was in not having your own people there and
depending on the neighborhood groups to generate your
crowd."

But the real problem with the meeting, Cortes explained, was
the situation in which they placed Mayor Cisneros. "He came to
the meeting for you—not for the neighborhood association.
And you should have protected him. He's got demands on his
time; he can't meet with every block association in town. Yet we
put him in a position where he had to agree to a meeting just to
get that neighborhood lady off the microphone. So, in a sense,
we let him down. After all, he meets with us because he needs
us, just like we need him. He needs us to do what we do because
it helps him keep the developers from running roughshod over
him . . . and the city. He can say to the developers, 'I've got
those crazy Mexicans on my tail, I can't let you do this or that.'

We understand this and can work with him. The neighborhood groups don't. They're in it for just one issue, for the short term, while we're going to be around a long time."

I remember that evaluation session vividly because it recalled for me the hundreds of frustrating and fruitless political meetings I had attended over 25 years. In my circles, we rarely made any kind of thoughtful analysis of our failures and certainly never worked through with our leaders any kind of understanding of how things might have been handled differently. We also rarely questioned how a meeting might relate to our long-range goals (did we have them?) or to our particular relationship with someone in power. In my politics—party politics, caucus politics, personality politics—if you learned, you learned on your own. If you challenged the leadership's ability to run the meeting, you had a bloodbath. If you admitted any sign of weakness, your cohorts would sprout vulture wings and circle in for the kill. And so when something went wrong, you picked a scapegoat or commiserated over a beer with a few trusted friends. Or, if it really mattered to you, you plotted a secretive action against your colleagues to wrest control of the organization for yourself and your cronies.

This was different. The evaluation was serious and supportive of the people who participated. There were no surprises or attacks. People were simply looking for a way to be more effective—individually and as an organization. They wanted to learn from their mistakes, take credit for their successes, and even accept responsibility for their failures. The process seemed not only to strengthen the men and women who participated, but to ensure the integrity of the organization as a whole.

One leader said of this kind of evaluation and soul-searching, "The blow-hards get weeded out real fast. . . . There is no place to hide."[9]

Maybe this is the accountability Cortes is talking about over lunch today. Maybe this is the safeguard against corruption. But Lefty Morris is not easily persuaded. "I'm beginning to think that even when we elect good people to office, they get so caught up in their need for flattery and attention that they lose sight of what is important," Morris says. "There is something in the political system itself that corrupts them. They just become useless and greedy."

"Some of them do," Cortes agrees. "But just as we know that power tends to corrupt, we also know that powerlessness corrupts. We've got a lot of people who've never developed an understanding of power. They've been institutionally trained to be passive. Power is nothing more than the ability to act in your own behalf, to act for your own interest."

"But people don't even know their own interests anymore," Morris insists.

"Unfortunately that is true," Cortes says. "But the only way we even *think* we can change this is by trying to teach about power and real self-interest. We get discouraged by the same things that bother you so we try to think in terms of long-term change. That's why we organize people around their values— not just issues. The issues fade and they lose interest. But what they really care about remains—family, dignity, justice, and hope. And we need power to protect what we value."

4

You Feel Like Your Work Is a Ministry

San Antonio, 1986

I drive for almost an hour through the suburbs and shopping centers in the rolling hills of northwest San Antonio before I find Mary and Jesse Moreno's home near the University of Texas Medical School. Jesse has worked for almost four years to remodel the white brick and frame house with bright blue shutters that sits on two acres in the tree-filled neighborhood. The house is spacious and comfortable for Mary and Jesse and their four children who range in age from 6 to 11. Wide windows bring in the pastoral scenes from the backyard where the children's pony grazes peacefully. While the kids watch Saturday morning cartoons in the den, Mary heats coffee in her microwave and we sit at a huge pine table in the dining room, where books and newspapers are stacked alongside children's art, school papers, and comfortable family clutter. The washing machine is humming in another room, and we hear Jesse hammering away, making repairs on the carport he recently added. Mary is telling me about her children with an enthusiasm that makes her seem younger than her 38 years. Her jet-black hair is cut stylishly short and she wears a diamond drop around her neck.

Mary Moreno has the confidence and grace of a seasoned politician, which is how her friends regarded her when she became an officer in the Metropolitan Congregational Alliance.[1] Trained by Ernesto Cortes and the Industrial Areas Foundation, Mary Moreno joined hundreds of new people moving into urban politics, disregarding the cynicism of media handlers and packaged candidates, and deciding to bring their own values to hardball political decision-making.

"My parents were victims," Mary tells me in her staccato voice only slightly tinged with a Spanish accent.[2] "We children were aware of the social injustices. We were migrant workers so we saw it all over. I remember the cotton pickings and everything. We went mostly to the Rio Grande Valley. We went to California and Michigan. But we always tried to get back so we kids could go to school. Sometimes we would have to stay until the crops were in and then we had to start school late. But we couldn't come home without any money. My mother had two years of school. My father had none."

Mary Moreno reminisces about the times in elementary school when there was neither food nor money in her house and she ate chewing gum for lunch, hoping the sugar would quell her stomach rumbles. She talks about the sweet sadness she saw in her father as he came home in despair with whiskey on his breath after being turned down for day labor, all day, every day for weeks. She talks about her older brothers and sisters dropping out of school to help support the family, and of her own determination to make something of herself, to finish high school, maybe even to go on to college after raising her own family.

"With all of this, two things stayed with me," she says. "One was the voting. Everyone was poor, but we were the poorest of the poor. One time my father came home, and he was very happy because he was able to get a dollar because a dollar was a lot of money. The way he got that dollar was that some patrón gave it to him for his vote. I didn't know about things like that at the time. I was only a little girl and we were just glad he could buy bread or flour or something. But it stayed with me. You know, who pays you for a vote? Every time there was an election, it was tamales and beer. Votes for the Mexicans. It always bothered me. I didn't know exactly why."

The other thing that stayed with Mary was her father's death.

"I had to fight the city and county, and I realized that things are not done because of right or wrong," she says. "It made me wake up."

In 1971, when she was 23 years old, Mary Moreno was a patients' representative at the Robert B. Green Hospital—San Antonio's charity facility. Her job included everything from helping police officers get information on stabbing victims to helping patients fill out forms to get a free shot for a baby with croup, or even translating into Spanish a doctor's explanation of an emergency surgical procedure that could save, or end, an old grandmother's life. Most of the patients at the Robert B. Green Hospital were Mexican-Americans, like Mary, who lived on the west side of Interstate 10. The highway split Anglo and Hispanic San Antonio into pieces almost as schizophrenic as geographic, making it difficult for anyone to conceive of the city as a whole. San Antonio was a divided culture, a divided economy, a divided people. Most men and women of Mexican ancestry lived west of the dividing line—the West Side. The old charity hospital, too, was on the West Side. And when the cultures of San Antonio met there, the mix was no less tense than in the city itself.

One of Mary Moreno's regular jobs at the hospital was to handle the paperwork for the bodies brought to the hospital's morgue over the weekend. It was routine: helping with identification, calling relatives, notifying priests. But Mary recalls that the morning of December 21 began differently. First, on her way to the morgue, she overheard a hospital orderly joking with a police guard about how they had "killed another Mexican" at the jail over the weekend. Then when she looked at the police report of the man brought in from the jail, she felt uneasy. "Latin male . . . about 60 . . . no identification . . . dead in cell . . . bruises. . . ."

Mary Moreno recalls placing her clipboard at the head of the stretcher, pulling back the sheet, and being startled by her own screams, which filled the morgue and spurted into the hospital halls like blood from a wound. The man under the sheet was her father!

Later, when her hysteria subsided, Mary was filled with questions. Why had her father been in jail? What had he done?

What had been done to him? Why were there bruises on his body? It was weeks before she began to get answers. And then, Mary did not like what she got.

The county medical examiner, a friend of hers, told Mary that her father had died from an attack of sclerosis of the liver. He had not been drunk when picked up on a West Side San Antonio street only three blocks from his home. But he had been semiconscious and disoriented from the concentration of liver bile building up in his system.

"The medical examiner told me, 'Mary, your dad was in the jail five hours before he died. He could have lived.' All that had to be done would have been to bring him to a hospital and pump him out and do a blood transfusion," she says. "Because of the way he was dressed—very simple with no shoes or socks—the police officer who found him thought he was drunk. Instead of taking him to the hospital, they took him to jail and put him in the drunk tank. I knew a lot of police officers and after I got hold of myself, I started finding out what happened."

A jail guard told Mary that one of the prisoners in the cell with her father was a mentally disturbed patient who had escaped from the state hospital. Police had picked him up and decided to leave him in jail overnight because they didn't want to drive across town to the state mental facility. The mental patient apparently assaulted Mary's father. As soon as the jail guards found Mary's father dead in the cell, the mental patient was whisked away to the hospital in the middle of the night. And the section of the police report detailing the injuries received by Mary's father was deleted after Mary had seen the initial report.

"Finding that out, I went crazy, screaming crazy again," Mary says. "I knew there was a cover-up and I had to stop them."

Mary confronted a police lieutenant who had been a friend of hers. "I told him there were procedures that should have been followed. Anytime you pick up someone who is hurt or unconscious, you are supposed to take them to the hospital first and then bring them to the jail. You even have a doctor in the jail and he examines them—but not even that happened to my father.

"Then the lieutenant told me, 'Well, Mary, if we had to take every disoriented bum we picked up to the Robert B. Green, we'd have to build at least three more charity hospitals just to hold them.'"

Mary Moreno was furious, and her anger spilled over like a boiling cauldron, burning everyone who got close. She saw lawyers, she badgered police officials, she called city council members and members of Congress. She harangued her friends. She became obsessive. She wanted an investigation, answers to her questions, justice for her father. But even though Mary persisted, she got nothing.

"I did everything wrong," she says. "The only thing I did right was to bother people about it. But I didn't know what I was doing. I just acted out of my anger."

After a while, previously friendly police officers began to shun her. Elected officials never returned her calls. Bureaucrats gave her the runaround. Lawyers told her to drop the matter. Her friends said she had done enough. And Mary and her family were exhausted by the ordeal.

"We were working alone. We had no strength, no power, nothing to help us. We were just one family," Mary says.

Mary Moreno's fury began to smolder when she realized she could do nothing to break the official silence that shrouded her father's death. "I didn't have the strength to see it through," she says. "Emotionally, I had to let it go. I went to visit my dad's grave and I let it go."

Then almost exactly 10 years later, it all came back to her.

In 1981, Mary Moreno's priest asked her to attend a meeting with representatives of other Catholic and Protestant churches on San Antonio's North Side, where a more prosperous Mary now lived with her husband and children. The church people wanted to organize themselves politically to improve neighborhoods whose main problem was the slow response time to their calls for police and fire protection. The organization was to be patterned after COPS, which was a church coalition of West Side Hispanic Catholics who had turned San Antonio politics upside down in the mid-1970s. Mary had always admired and laughed at the confrontational antics of COPS, as its members disrupted city council meetings with stinging satirical skits and pokes at unresponsive public officials. Because the organization could turn out as many as 50,000 West Side votes on election day, it generated fear among city officials who endured its infamous accountability sessions. But working-class families looked at COPS with awe because for the first time in the history of the city, they had access to its decision-making structure. COPS became the dominant force in city politics, its members proudly wearing their red, white, and blue COPS lapel buttons, even instructing relatives to make sure they would be buried with them when the time came. COPS dramatically changed San Antonio, making it more open, more fun, and more responsive to the needs of people who lived on the West Side. Now, even some North Side churches seemed to be infected with the COPS spirit.

"I don't even remember the specific discussion, only that there were about 15 people from each parish who came together at this meeting of delegates," Mary tells me. "The leaders were stressing the importance of getting together the laypeople in each church and developing them to work together for justice. At the meeting something happened to me . . . all of my memories just came back to me at once: my father, being poor, the frustration, my helplessness. Here was something I didn't know how to do, and they were offering me the chance to learn."

Mary Moreno jumped at the chance. That it was offered to her in her neighborhood parish, the prosperous St. Brigid's Catholic Church on the North Side of San Antonio, was a reflection of how far-reaching the effect of COPS had been—not only on poor people on the West Side of San Antonio, but on both Catholic and Protestant churches all over the country that believed that their mission had to include a commitment to God and neighbor. COPS seemed to Mary to offer that commitment. If MCA could be like COPS, then she would sign on.

About 17 people from Mary's parish began attending the training sessions that would show them how to develop political skills. Mary learned how to get public information about issues and problems, how to prepare for a public meeting, how to plot strategy, how to confront a public official, how to get the news media interested—all of the skills that would have helped her 10 years earlier. She was excited by the possibilities.

"I would take people from the church to the meetings and then go back to educate those who couldn't go," Mary says. "We found that there was a lot of interest. But a big question kept coming up: Why is the church getting involved in things like this?"

Mary Moreno says she thought about it a lot. She remembered how her Catholic faith had grasped and comforted her through the hard times in her life. Now that her life was full—a home, a family, a hope for the future—that faith seemed to require her to act for others whose lives did not seem so full. She began to look on MCA as her own very special kind of service to people like her father and mother, like her old neighbors on the West Side.

"What is the church if it is not helping people?" she asks. "I see it as hypocrisy if you go pray for an hour on Sunday, then come home and watch television and say 'to hell with my neighbor.'

"I guess I have a lot to learn," Mary laughs to break the seriousness of the mood and cool the anger that has crept into her tone. "But I care too much about the followers, the nobodies," she continues, letting her passion build once again. "When I see someone alone in a group, someone nobody's talking to, I go up and talk to them. That's who we should be working for. What you go through when you're a nobody and don't have any status or money made me realize that you need to be together with other people to have some kind of power.

"I am still angry," Mary says reflectively as we sip our coffee amid the hum of her domestic life. And then she smiles as if to let me in on a secret, and with the arch of an eyebrow she says, "But I'm learning to use my anger."

For Mary Moreno, that meant learning how to turn her hot burning anger down a notch or two and make it cold, controlled, and careful, guiding it like some swift, sure missile homing in on its target—the school board that lets a neighborhood school deteriorate, the industrial polluter that is ruining the water supply, the police department that looks the other way when teenage gangs terrorize the neighborhood. With her new cold anger, Mary Moreno says, "You don't feel like you're a radical. You really feel like your work is a ministry."[3]

5

The University of COPS

San Antonio, 1986

The doors to the old elementary school on the grounds of the Immaculate Heart of Mary parish on the West Side of San Antonio are locked. Only the small red, white, and blue lapel button taped over a doorbell gives me any assurance that I am where I want to be: at the office of the neighborhood organization COPS. A hand-lettered sign lets me know I must ring the bell to gain entrance. The parish and the West Side neighborhood are so poor and devastated by urban renewal that they can no longer support the school. So the 70-year-old building is locked, boarded up, and used only for periodic sessions of an adult literacy class—and for the COPS headquarters, located on the second floor and accessible to the West Side leaders who run the organization. After my first visit, I understood the necessity of the locked doors. There are hazards in the old building and in the neighborhood. One day I lost my footing and fell on a chipped cement stairway that had no railings. Another time, a mentally retarded man exposed himself to me in the parking lot.

Today, it is only cold, and as I look through old clippings and files, I huddle close to the small space heater in one of the three rooms COPS uses for offices and meetings. The visible signs of COPS' power show not in the office, but in the expandable files of newspaper clippings that grow larger with each passing year. The headlines mark the progress:

> 1976—"Rebuilding is Central Demand of COPS," San Antonio *Express*;
> 1977—"COPS Denies Disruption," San Antonio *Light*;
> 1981—"COPS Plans Meeting with Power Brokers," San Antonio *Light*;
> 1983—"Governor Makes Pledge to COPS," San Antonio *News*;
> 1985—"COPS Budget $150,000," San Antonio *Express*; and it goes on.

I have been working in the files for about an hour when I am called to the telephone. It is Ernie Cortes calling from Austin. I am surprised because I had not mentioned to him that I would be in San Antonio, but he tracked me down anyway to ask, "Are you finding anything interesting?"

It was a question Cortes asked me frequently during my intermittent research and review of his organizations. And it was his way of keeping tabs on what I was hearing and thinking about them. The questions, daily telephone calls, and continuous dialogue—not only with me, but with dozens of other people—are his way of keeping up with what is happening within each organization. He talks with his paid organizers and key volunteer leaders almost everyday. He asks about everything they do—from their appointments, to the size of the banners for their rallies, to their impressions of a visit with a city council member, even to the current books they are reading. I should have guessed that Cortes would find my tracks wherever I went within the network. He seemed to be everywhere and into everything. One of his full-time organizers, Sister Maribeth Larkin, told me once, "We operate out of Ernie's vision."[1] Although Cortes discounts this and credits his organizers for helping develop a "shared" vision, he nevertheless keeps his hand in every activity in every organization.

I spent an hour at his Austin office one afternoon watching him work the telephone to get the help of Victoria's Catholic Bishop Charles Grahmin[2] for a pet project and prepare—via a conference call—his leaders in San Antonio and the Rio Grande Valley for a meeting on economic development with then–San Antonio Mayor Henry Cisneros. A few minutes later he was delegating tasks to Austin organizer Ken Fujimoto for a meeting on affordable housing with Admiral Bobby Ray Inman, the former CIA operative and high-tech entrepreneur. In the middle of all of this, he took a call from Duke University's Larry Goodwyn, the historian of populism and author of *Democratic Promise,* and he advised Goodwyn to read Pope John Paul's papal encyclical on work, *Laborem Excerens,* in order to understand the Polish pope and the Catholic church as background for Goodwyn's forthcoming book on the Solidarity movement.

It was a dizzying experience to be with Cortes in his office. Often, his two young children Jacob and Alma would be there. Cortes regularly took over baby-sitting chores so that his wife Oralia could work on her degree in library science. Sometimes Ami, his teenaged daughter from his first marriage, would also be there answering the telephone for him or filing the news clips on key issues or Industrial Areas Foundation activities. His son Jacob, then 5 years old, would crawl up in his father's lap or beg for a sip of Cortes' ever-present diet soft drink, and Cortes would tell him, "Son, you know it's bad for you." Jacob would retort, "But *you* do it, dad." And Alma, three years older than her brother, would look up from her book and roll her eyes, as if to say, "Well, here we go again." Then Cortes would shift his attention to her, to her books: "Are you reading anything interesting, Alma? Tell me what you're reading." Later, he would recount with delight stories of Alma's passion for books, which, of course, mirrored his own.

I was never around Cortes when he was not simultaneously reading five or six books—mostly theology, history, economics, and biography. Books were everywhere around him—his office, car, home, garage. When Cortes' wife Oralia was packing to move into a new home, she complained to me that she had found more than 30 unpacked boxes of books from their last move. And that reminded Cortes to tell me about his recent readings from the half-dozen books he was carrying in a canvas bag, and to offer me two of them: a book on Catholic social teachings and another on the role of leadership in effective management.

As often happened with Cortes, one book led to an idea,

which resulted in a search for another book among those stacked to double depth on the shelves lining the walls of his small Austin office. Which also had newspapers stacked on the floor—the *Wall Street Journal, New York Times, Christian Science Monitor, Dallas Morning News,* and others—waiting to be clipped for his files. To keep up with Cortes, I found that my own reading expanded into areas in which I had never ventured before—particularly into economics, philosophy, and theology. He seemed eager for me to read, eager to show me the intellectual path to his own development so that I could better understand why and how he had come to build the organizations in the way he had.

Cortes clearly loved to teach. Once he was finally able to recruit and train enough organizers in Texas to share the tedium of daily organizing duties, he began to put together seminars and training classes that stretched his leaders intellectually and created what one of his organizers called a "community of scholars." In fact, Cortes began to look at his organizations as a mini-university. "It is a place where people learn . . . where people are really thinking about politics in an interesting way, about economics and other disciplines. Where they are trying to apply what they learn," Cortes explains. "What we want are organizers and leaders who really understand reflection and see themselves as scholars who synthesize reading, reflection, and action. Our role is not merely to help. It is easy to encourage dependency. Our role is to teach. It's hard to do, to keep up the energy for it, but I think it is essential."[3]

Community leader and former COPS president Helen Ayala said that when she completed her term of office, she felt as if she had graduated from the "University of COPS." Bill Eassum, pastor of the Colonial Hills Methodist Church in San Antonio, believed the training he received was more "profound" than anything he had learned in three years at the Perkins School of Theology.

Former *Texas Observer* editor Geoffrey Rips says the realization that Cortes was teaching as well as organizing sent him reeling: "The sphere of politics was suddenly much larger. It was not only a place to act but also a place to think. The importance of politicians and the electoral apparatus shrank in comparison to the development of people Cortes called 'leaders,' all those who are engaged simultaneously in the restructuring of power relationships and in the development of their own understanding and that of others."[4]

Philosophers Hannah Arendt and José Ortega y Gasset turned up on Cortes' reading lists, along with political scientist Bernard Crick, economist Lester Thurow, and theologians Walter Brueggemann, Hans Kung, Gregory Baum, and Leonardo Boff. Cortes urged IAF leaders to read biographies to learn how power and leadership developed through individual lives. Disraeli, Churchill, Huey Long, Robert Moses, Martin Luther King, Jr., Lyndon B. Johnson—even J. Edgar Hoover—became points of reference in his lectures. So did church documents.

For six weeks in 1985, Valley Interfaith met every Sunday for four hours to study Pope John Paul's encyclical on work and the American Catholic Bishops' Letter on the Economy. More than 1,500 people went through the courses, and the collective decision of the organization to lobby in Austin for indigent health-care legislation came out of these meetings.

Other seminar topics included ideas about the concept of the public good, trade and monetary policy, and the United States' relationship with Mexico. And power. Always back to power.

Power as seen by Lord Acton: "Power tends to corrupt, and absolute power corrupts absolutely."[5]

Power as seen by Catholic theologian Hans Kung: "The exercise of power . . . can be justified in virtue of service and must be judged by its character as service."[6]

Power as seen by the patron saint of community organizers, Saul Alinsky: "Power is the very essence, the dynamo of life. It is the power of the heart pumping blood and sustaining life in the body. It is the power of active citizen participation, pulsing upward, providing a unified strength for a common purpose."[7]

The full range of power is a hard concept to grasp if you have never exercised it, and Cortes returns to it repeatedly to train people to use it for broad social purposes. Ed Chambers, the IAF's national director, said that in the early days of COPS, Cortes had to go in several times to admonish its leaders and tell them, "Hey, this is not about some Mexicans getting some power. This concept is bigger than that."[8]

So Cortes talks frequently with his leaders about the ambiguities of power—about the kind of power that tends to corrupt and the kind of power than comes from knowledge. He believes that knowledge can be the path to power for people within its organizations.

"Power ultimately depends on consent," he says. "And we're teaching how you go about getting consent. The problem in government is how you delegate the work to the experts, the professionals and bureaucrats, without delegating the power. We want people to become expert enough to challenge the experts and maintain the power all the while."

Cortes says he also returns to power again and again in his workshops because many of the church members who make up his organizations are uncomfortable with the idea of power. He tries to get them to separate power from brute force and violence and to look at it in terms of cooperation rather than coercion. Cortes gets his leaders to read Protestant theologian Paul Tillich's book *Love, Power and Justice* because Tillich believes that love and power have to be joined to produce justice. "Tillich talks about how love without power leads to sentimentality, while power without love leads to cynicism. You have to operate with both and it creates a tension that's not always comfortable," Cortes says.

"We had people analyze their own experience with power one time, and it was usually bad because they were on the short end of it," he says. "They simply never had the joy of exercising it! We just want them to have a little joy."

6

Anger Gives You Energy

Los Angeles, 1986

"Pastor Sinnott, please leave the room and wait in the hall!"

Edward T. Chambers, teacher, issues the command, and the Reverend Thomas Sinnott, student, follows it.

Chambers, director of the Industrial Areas Foundation, is teaching a seminar on power at Mount St. Mary's College in the hills overlooking Los Angeles. Tom Sinnott is a Lutheran minister from New Jersey, and he is one of about 100 people from across the nation who are attending the IAF's training program for church leaders and community activists.[1]

During the next 10 minutes, Chambers orders other people to leave the room as well—a youth gang social worker from East Los Angeles, a school teacher from El Paso, a lawyer from East Brooklyn, a Methodist minister from St. Louis. All obey the order. After all, Chambers is the head guy, the leader, the man in charge of the program. But the program is about power, and about how most middle-class and poor people give consent to have it taken away from them.

"We teach not only how to get power, but how to use it," Chambers begins.

All eyes are on Ed Chambers, who dominates the room physically as well as emotionally. In his 50s, tall and barrel-chested, Chambers has the stiff-necked posture of intense pride. When he lectures, he sometimes calls forth a moral authority gleaned from his studies with the Benedictines at St. John's College. Or, if it seems to work better, he falls back on plain old street-smarts, picked up from almost 30 years of organizing poor people in the slums of Chicago, New York City, Rochester, and other places. His scowl is so deliberate that it looks like he paints it across his face for effect. But there are flickers of warmth beneath his severity, and when he smiles he can't keep from looking like kindly Robert Young in *Father Knows Best*, who becomes stern and authoritative only because he has to teach young Bud and Kitten the difference between right and wrong. Or, in Chambers' case with this class, the difference between power and powerlessness.

"The only purpose of our organization is to amass power—but we are not interested in brute power . . . we are about relational power," he says. "There is a difference between strength and bullying. Power can afford to be practical, flexible, wise, patient. Power can administer justice. When you have power, you can afford to be generous. Power moves orderly; it doesn't crush. The misuse of power sets the seed of its own destruction.

"The drive for power and love come with becoming a whole person. Love is needed to be, but power is needed to act. We give away our power by consenting to people who act like they have authority."

For Pastor Sinnott, standing outside the door and straining to hear the lecture, an electric flash of insight rushes through the circuits of his brain. Why is he standing in the hallway while everyone else is participating in the lecture? Why did he, an ordained minister, automatically accept Chambers' command to leave the room? For what purpose? And who the hell is Ed Chambers, anyway! An enraging click of awareness propels the minister back into the classroom, and Ed Chambers, with a smile breaking across his face, stops his lecture as Tom Sinnott enters the room.

"Congratulations, Pastor Sinnott," Chambers bellows as the minister reclaims his chair, his gaze fixed suspiciously on Chambers who is in turn searching the faces of the people in his classroom, waiting to see if they understand what is happening. Then he addresses them.

"What you have seen is someone taking charge of his life; you have seen courage, even a revolutionary act. Pastor Sinnott is changing history by taking action. He is changing what is happening to us here and now. That's just what Rosa Parks did when she kicked off the whole civil rights movement by seizing what was rightfully hers—the right to choose where to sit on the bus in Montgomery, Alabama," Chambers says. "She broke a habit of unquestioning acquiescence to authority that robbed her of her dignity and rights. That took courage, and courage marks the beginning of power."

The men and women who sit in the classroom are smiling now, and the other people Chambers had ordered from the room sheepishly return.

"We have created a teachable moment about power here today. This is how we learn," Chambers says. "We make people act it out. We play roles. As you play the role is how you are at home. It is a mirror for you. Because all of us are so trained to give consent to authority, I probably could have emptied the room a few minutes ago. Because I assumed an authoritative role, you handed over your power to me. If Pastor Sinnott had not acted, there is no telling what I might have done to you."

Chambers is obviously delighted with the minister. Not all of his classes get the point, and many times in his training sessions several people spend the entire hour standing in the hall. Yet what happened today is what he strives for—a personal and direct experience that cannot be doubted. And the telling and retelling of personal experiences—both of power and powerlessness—is the way people come to understand what happens to them and why.

"We are trained to give consent to people in authority. First it is our parents, then teachers, then bosses and politicians," he explains. "But when you become mature, when you are informed, when you know yourself, you begin to take responsibility for your own actions and you begin to make decisions about when you will and will not consent to someone else's power. Our society is based on informed consent of *all* the people. We play by the rules when we have the chance to participate in making them. But when we've been left out of the rule-making and when authority is used arbitrarily against us to shut us out or deprive us of what we need to live, we can withdraw our consent . . . we can begin to amass our own power to change the rules. Some in religion may call it spirit—the holy spirit. But I call it power. God gave us this power over our lives. It is a gift, and we shouldn't give it away to others."

During the week I spend in Los Angeles with Ed Chambers, Ernie Cortes, and other IAF members, they create a number of "teachable" moments—direct experiences—about power, the nature of politics, the importance of relationships, and the uses of anger. All are designed to bring home to people the importance of taking responsibility for their actions—of looking deeply enough into themselves to develop the courage necessary to seek power. The Iron Rule—never doing for people what they can do for themselves—is central to the training.

"I enjoy seeing people who don't have anything get something. I like to see it in their eyes," says a young black man at the training session who runs a church-based charity in Mississippi.

But most people who express this well-intentioned feeling for others don't have the slightest idea what to do about it. And so, with the best of intentions, they act *for* people instead of teaching people how to act for themselves. This is where the IAF networks in Texas, California, New York, Maryland, and other states seem to differ from hundreds of other community organizations that have sprouted from the same motivational seeds. The IAF organizations concentrate on the development of skill and insight that allows people to act for themselves, to transform themselves from passive participants who are content to have things done for them into actors who initiate change in their inner as well as outer lives. This transformation of inner attitudes and behavior seems to be critical to the success and longevity of the IAF organizations.

For every public event where the purpose of the organization is to get a specific result—a rally to lobby a local city council to put a fire station in a neighborhood of modest homes, or a delegation of leaders who meet with the mayor about moving the location of a municipal airport—there may be dozens of private sessions to learn, analyze, and understand what might occur and why, and what it might mean on both a personal and political level for the people who participate. It is a very thoughtful process and one in which consequences of political behavior are carefully weighed in terms of broad social goals,

deeply felt values, and personal growth. The training sometimes even moves to a deep personal level that forces people to
confront and know themselves as a prerequisite to confronting
politicians and becoming effective in the political process.
Occasionally, that kind of training can be downright uncomfortable.

In one classroom at Mount St. Mary's, Ernie Cortes has asked
two ministers, one white and one black, to sit in front of a group
of 30 people and conduct a "role-play." Their task is to practice
a "one-on-one" meeting, the technique used to recruit new leaders and get church people involved in the organization. The
major purpose of the recruitment meeting is to establish a personal relationship with a potential leader, to find out what the
individual really cares about, and to show him or her that there
might be an effective way to get it through the political process.

The black minister has a wide white mane of hair with matching whiskers that gives him a certain dignity even while dressed
in his Bermuda shorts and white Reeboks. The young white
minister looks less like a man of the cloth than a serious be-
spectacled graduate student at home in the college atmosphere.
They begin their conversation awkwardly; it is hard to initiate
a private conversation in front of 30 political activists and
clergy, and particularly in front of Cortes. But the two men
gradually overcome the strange role-play aspects of their situation. They begin by talking about their common frustrations
with the ministry and the admonitions from the Bible they are
trying to follow. It is slow, theological—and surprisingly superficial. But after five minutes, they seem to forget the people in
the classroom and concentrate on each other.

"When you stand to preach Sunday after Sunday, you feel
like the surgeon who performs perfect surgery, but the patient
dies," says the black minister. "My powerlessness as a pastor . . .
the powerlessness of the people I preach to is so frustrating. I
struggle to make the gospel live, to become actual in peoples'
lives rather than to operate under doctrines and principles that
have no life."

Then the white minister begins to talk about the incidents in
his life when he could not connect with the God he tries to
serve. It was not in church, he admits, but in ordinary situations, such as sitting at the kitchen table, trying to comfort

someone in trouble and realizing that the problems were beyond his capability to solve. He confesses his powerlessness to help.

"All week long during this training, I've flashed back to times, incidents when it could have been different if I had known what to do," he says. "Somebody's child can't read, and you go to school with the parent to see if you can help, but it's too late to help because something should have been done years ago and you only touch one part of the system. You try to be effective and you can't be. You invest energy and you don't get anywhere. It hurts."

The conversation suddenly becomes personal, and the pastor's hurt shows in his eyes and softens his voice. People in the classroom are quiet, struggling to understand the emotions unleashed as the pastor moves from theological generalities to the specifics of his feelings. He has provided an opening to himself—a vulnerability—that allows us to feel what he feels and perhaps to understand something of his nature. And sitting there in the classroom, we realize that this kind of opening could allow a connection with him to develop, perhaps the beginnings of a relationship.

The opening of "self" by this pastor paves the way for another glimpse into the one-on-one process in the next role-play Cortes arranges. This time, the participants are a young black teacher disillusioned with her career in the Los Angeles schools and a prominent black Methodist minister from Houston. Again, the role-play starts on a superficial level. Then the self-possessed stylish woman begins to provide some clues about herself and her frustrations that indicate she might be ready to open up, to establish a connection. But the minister doesn't follow up. He carefully withholds even the smallest hint of his own feelings and is almost unresponsive to the teacher. The role-play is on the verge of breaking down when Cortes intervenes. In a gentle voice, he asks the minister if he would be willing to tell the group about his son.

And the minister, whose physical bulk might enable him to go straight from his Sunday pulpit to the Astrodome to play linebacker for the Houston Oilers, snaps to attention as if Cortes had sneaked up on him and yelled "gotcha!" Then, his shoulders drop and he takes a deep breath, shifting in his chair and looking Cortes directly in the eyes. He begins speaking softly, with obvious resignation. "I have a 6-year-old son who had meningitis when he was 5 months old, and he can't speak or dress himself now."

The impact of the minister's simple, sad words on the people in the room is stunning. For me, this man's imposing bulk and bearing seem inconsequential now that I've witnessed his distress. He struggles to continue speaking, and his voice slowly picks up volume and force. "I'm angry," he says. "And I have to wrestle with the fact that this happened to me. I don't like this feeling. I've got to channel this feeling into something constructive."

The young teacher in the role-play gropes for something to say. "Did you get involved in this kind of political organizing because you wanted to feel victorious about something?" she asks.

"Hell, no!" the minister shouts. "I don't need victories. I get victory every Sunday when I walk away from the pulpit. What I want is to do something about this feeling of being power- less . . . for myself . . . for others."

Cortes steps into the center of the room and focuses all of his attention on the minister. "Who do you get angry with?" he asks.

The minister hesitates, looks at the ceiling and all around the room, anywhere but at Cortes. He scrunches up his face and finally mutters an almost inaudible reply. "The power structure . . . the corporations . . ."

"What do you mean?" shouts Cortes incredulously. "The corporations didn't give your child meningitis!" Then, more softly and very deliberately, he adds, "When I was a child and my sister died, I didn't get angry with the corporations, I got angry with God!"

Quietly, with a half-smile on his face, the minister nods in recognition. "I guess I've cursed Him once or twice," he says. "Then I have to turn around and proclaim Him on Sunday."

"That's hard, isn't it?" Cortes comments.

"Yes, it's hard."

The room is silent.

"But I was lucky," the minister begins speaking again, softly talking about the practical problems of raising a handicapped child. "I had insurance. But now when I go with other families to the hospital with their children, and they don't have any money, that's when I really get angry with the doctors and the politicians."

"Well, pastor," Cortes says, "anger gives you energy."

"But I don't need a cannon to kill a mosquito."

All of us are silent as we leave the classroom. I wonder about this exchange. What am I really seeing? What does it mean? Why does the minister's doubt express something more spiritual to me than certainty? Why does it have such power? And why do I have the urge at this moment to act, to make it right when someone else has been wronged? And why do most of us leaving this room seem to share these feelings?

If you take part in the kinds of political organizing proposed by Ernesto Cortes, do you have to go deeply into yourself, to take emotional risks with others in order to be certain about the changes you want to bring about in the life of the community, to right the wrongs? Is it more than mere politics?

In the hallway, I overhear the comment of a middle-aged man from New York whom I had been watching during the session. He is a veteran political organizer from the old days with Saul Alinsky in Chicago and New York. Because of his reputation and demeanor, I judged him an indifferent sophisticate, a knowledgeable cynic, a political skeptic like myself. Then I hear his voice shape words I had not heard in years.

"I think we've just seen the holy spirit at work."

7

The First Revolution Is Internal

Austin, 1986

I wait for Sister Christine Stephens in the coffee shop at the Ramada Inn, one block from the State Capitol building. She is about 20 minutes late for our appointment, and when she finally arrives, it is only to pause long enough to apologize for the delay of her airplane and to excuse herself for a few minutes more to make a telephone call. The call is to check with the lieutenant governor's office about his itinerary for an upcoming tour of the *colonias* in the Rio Grande Valley. Lieutenant Governor William P. Hobby Jr. wants officials from the state's water agencies to see the neighborhoods where people live without adequate water and sewer systems, and Stephens is making arrangements for the trip. But at the last minute, Governor Mark White, who is facing a stiff challenge to his reelection bid, decides he wants to go along.[1] And now, with the governor's staff and press entourage, arrangements have to be made for 50 people. What started out as a simple visit by water officials has turned into a political circus, which Stephens must manage. As I watch the tall, no-nonsense, graying woman in a blue business suit, there is no doubt in my mind that she can handle it.

Christine Stephens is an anomaly—a Catholic nun turned political organizer. She and at least four other sisters from religious orders are among the dozen full-time paid organizers who recruit and train leaders for the Industrial Areas Foundation organizations in Texas. Stephens has worked with organizations in Houston and San Antonio and has primary responsibility now for Valley Interfaith. Like all IAF organizers, Stephens' task is to identify potential leaders from local churches and work with them to develop public skills and private self-confidence. Another major task is to help those leaders develop a political strategy that will build the power of their organizations and help make the changes local residents feel necessary to improve their lives. Stephens' reputation as a skilled organizer and strategist prompts our meeting today. In her mid-40s, Stephens is one of the senior IAF-trained organizers in the nation and is a formidable presence in Texas.

I understand that in the IAF jargon, Stephens and I are about to have a one-on-one, which means that there is motivation and purpose behind what appears to be a simple conversation between two women over coffee on a spring afternoon. I want Stephens to give me information about Ernesto Cortes and his organizations in Texas, and she wants to find out from me how her groups are perceived by the politicians I know. Because we are both deeply involved in Texas politics and know that our paths are likely to cross again, we each want to be comfortable with the other. We want to establish between us some basis for trust, some private relationship that can be the foundation for future involvement.

Stephens speaks slowly and deliberately, reflecting her caution about consequences—any consequences stemming from any action. The caution is the seed of her strength as a strategist and her weakness as a quick initiator of action, she claims. "To be an organizer or a leader in our effort, you have to initiate relationships. You have to see yourself as the actor always and never as the passive person," Stephens says.[2]

Christine Stephens is comfortable with her role as an organizer, as an initiator of relationships. But in 1976 when she began this kind of work, she felt awkward and unsure about her ability to extend herself. "I didn't understand it and I didn't think I could do it. I couldn't even tell people I was an organizer. I couldn't get the word out of my mouth," she says, making a face and laughing. "When I first started as a leader,

I remember being frightened out of my wits. I didn't know how to get out of myself. I was too stiff. I had a certain image of myself. I've been a nun 24 years. I'm through and through a nun. When I went into the order, we were still wearing long skirts and habits. We were taught the demeanor and conduct of a proper nun. We were taught how to walk, how to swing our arms, how to walk down stairs in long habits."

Stephens was 23 years old when she entered the Community of Divine Providence religious order. As a social worker, she concentrated on poor members of Catholic parishes, and when she first met Ernesto Cortes, she headed the local office of a Catholic charity, the Campaign for Human Development, which was operated by Houston's Catholic Diocese. Some of Houston's Catholic and Protestant church members had just formed The Metropolitan Organization (TMO) and had hired Cortes to help achieve for Houston's poor what COPS had accomplished in San Antonio. Stephens was serving as chair of the local sponsoring committee, and Cortes quickly spotted her leadership potential. He began working with her to develop it.

"We had a hard session one time about my leadership style, how I made a presentation in public, how I came across to people. No one had ever done that with me before. I hated it, but I wanted to learn those things. I was scared stiff and Ernie had to push me," Stephens remembers.

Cortes gave her books to read on power and philosophy, public policy and politics. He also kept pushing her deeper into herself to understand how and why she operated as she did. What began to impress Christine Stephens about Cortes and the IAF was that for the first time in her life, someone valued and respected her anger. Although she was a nun to her core, Stephens was also an angry woman, once disrupting a meeting of Tenneco shareholders to protest the $1.25 hourly wage paid to farmworkers on lands owned by the company. Her sense of righteous indignation was aroused by the slightest hint of unfairness, and she waged a continuing war with herself to keep her temper from triggering her tongue.

Christine Stephens grew up in a working-class family in Houston where her father was a union pipefitter and her mother struggled with debilitating rheumatoid arthritis that destroyed her body and sapped the family's spirit. Life centered around Stephens' ailing mother, who grew weaker and weaker, her bones literally crumbling within her frail body. "My mother had been a beautiful woman, but toward the end of her life even her jaw bones began to disintegrate. She lived through a mastectomy and a heart attack, but she had tremendous courage. She also had a terrific temper that seemed to keep her going," Stephens says.

Mother and daughter shared that temper, and they frequently had tremendous rows. The young Christine would argue to exhaustion for what she considered right.

"My anger probably comes from the way my family handled the emotional aspects of my mother's illness," she says. "There was a lot of denial. As my mother got worse, my dad took early retirement to take care of her. He felt that his sheer will power could keep her going. And when she finally died, he was so hurt because he couldn't save her. He was just devastated by her death."

The pressures that bound Stephens to her family were economic as well as emotional. She wanted to attend the University of Texas at Austin, but the family could not afford it so Stephens lived at home while on a scholarship to Houston's University of St. Thomas.

"My family lived in the same house off Telephone Road in southeast Houston for 40 years," Stephens says. "We had three cars over a lifetime. We bought things to keep for life. When the next-door neighbors moved out of the neighborhood for a better house, my mother had such contempt for them. That kind of quest for better things was not part of our lives."

As Sister Christine Stephens talks about her family, fears, and aspirations, I realize that with the exposure of her vulnerability, she is providing an opening to me, an invitation for me to see "inside" the strong self-confident woman across the table, and to understand that it has not been an easy transition for her from daughter to nun to political player. But the invitation is also for me to respond with some hint of my own vulnerability so that she can better understand me, and that is hard for me to do. I am like most people, who clam up and change the subject when strangers come too close to long-hidden feelings and fears. Yet in the conversation with this Catholic nun, the process of intimate paring and probing is not invasive. It is selective and sensitive, probing rather than prying. It is like maneuvering a freshly crafted key into a door lock, which, when it fits, seems to open you as well as the other person. As Christine Stephens talks, I feel that I know her in ways I fail to know friends of 20 years. I realize how meetings like this develop relationships and alliances, how they provide an essential human connection that is necessary to build an enduring political connection. In an informal, unstructured way, it is what people always do when they build relationships based on shared aspirations and experiences. The IAF one-on-one is merely a systematic way of organizing this process.

In the IAF organizations, one-on-one meetings like this are used initially to recruit new leaders, to get church people to work with others for political action. The major purpose is to show potential leaders that there might be a better way to achieve the things they care about deeply. But discovery of the depth of that caring has to come first, and a special kind of person is the target.

Organizers like Christine Stephens look for people who are rooted in the community—not self-appointed leaders such as social workers or low-grade politicians—but layleaders in church organizations, the PTAs, school, or service groups. They seek people who have already demonstrated in other settings a capacity for leadership, a concern for others, and a vision that would allow them to risk change. Once identified, organizers meet individually with these men and women and listen to them. It is a process akin to courting.

"The purpose of the initial one-on-one contacts with potential leaders is not so much to sell them on us, but merely to propose that they look at us and consider the possibility of a relationship with us," Ernesto Cortes says. "When you sell, you tend to be arrogant. You know it all. You build up yourself and you quit listening. You're not attentive."

In proposing, rather than selling, Cortes believes you have to have flexibility, curiosity, patience, and a little vulnerability. And that involves some self-revelation as well as propositioning. The best organizers and leaders learn how to reveal themselves in small doses as part of the process of drawing out others, as Christine Stephens does with me. The successful one-on-one becomes a give-and-take relationship, not a one-sided interview.

The process of relationship building within a political context did not develop overnight. "We did one-on-ones early in COPS, but they were different," Cortes says. "Sometimes it would work and sometimes it wouldn't. And I didn't know what made it work or not . . . I was still in uncharted territory as far as thinking it out and working it out for myself."

But in the years since 1973, when Cortes started COPS, the one-on-one has become a fully analyzed tool within the IAF. "You don't just discuss what people do, or their ideology or the theology of their actions," according to Cortes. "You must go deeper. Ultimately you must get to the level of how people *feel* about what they do. You want to understand the sources of their anger, or their love, or their interest in something beyond themselves."

Even after church members decide to take an active part in the organizations, the relationship building continues, much like a slow, steady rain that smoothes the rocky rough edges of emotional and political inexperience.

Mary Moreno tells of coming home from an MCA meeting one evening to find her telephone ringing off the wall. It was MCA organizer Tim McClusky, who peppered her with questions about the meeting and the role she had played in it. How did she think it went? How did she feel about what she said? Is this the direction she felt the organization should take?

"Tim would push me a lot . . . he'd hear me out and cause me to think about how I felt," Mary says. "Then he would talk about the bigger picture and how it all fit. He was teaching. He took the time. I could go back to him later with questions or ideas. But you can't do that with organizers unless you've built the relationship first."[3]

This belief in relationships, in a form of personal nurturing in a safe setting, permeates activities among organizers, leaders, and followers within the IAF organizations. "The organization provides a way to grow and develop," Ed Chambers believes. "You have to be nurtured to survive. But we've devised a one-on-one relationship meeting where the purpose is public business. If you become a key leader, I promise we will help you to organize, to get up and speak before 2,000 people or do a press interview and feel good about yourself and have the organization think you did a good job."

The responsible use of public skills, then, stems not only from the self-confidence that comes from mastering the techniques, but from a self-knowledge and connection with other people that is designed to show leaders how relationships work with each other, and with those who hold power.

But where does it all lead?

"The personal growth and development of people is why we do what we do," Chambers stresses. "That's what broad-based organizations do for people—change their lives and integrate their values and vision. The first revolution is internal. It requires commitment to operate on your center."

A significant amount of time and energy in the IAF national training programs is devoted to inciting the first revolution— the internal one that comes with an awareness of self and self-worth. And flowing naturally from that is the focus on individual relationship building. People who have a strong sense of self can afford to take the risks involved in relationship building. The IAF attempts to provide the skills to do just that, but what people learn instead of rules and procedures is how to be flexible, conversational, and insightful. It is almost like good therapy—slow and difficult. And successful, only if you work at it. It is also incredibly frustrating for people who believe that politics must be all action.

As Cortes was explaining the one-on-one in a training session one day, an impatient young man from Baltimore began to complain. "I take all of this talk for granted. Let's get down to the business of organizing," he admonished Cortes.

Visibly angered, Cortes spun around and thrust himself in the young man's face and shouted, "But this *is* it! It is all here. This is the action. This is the test of whether or not we're doing what we say we are. This is where you learn it all. *This is all we have to offer!*"

Then Cortes backed away and began to explain. "If we don't go anywhere, it's because these one-on-ones don't develop. Organizers burn out if they don't do individual meetings. Pastors lose interest if they don't do this. This is where the spiritual action is. We didn't invent it. It's been done from time immemorial. Part of *being* is the ability to share ourselves—it is part of our personal grounding for public action. It is not just what we think, but what we feel. It's getting to the roots of our personal being."

For IAF leaders, the root of "personal being" is not only understanding feelings in themselves and others, but in coming to terms with their own fundamental self-interest, and then learning to act on it. "Self-interest requires that you recognize yourself, that you say 'I count,'" Ed Chambers believes.

The concept of self-interest that Cortes and Chambers talk about was initially a source of confusion to me. I kept thinking about selfishness and special-interest groups in politics, which push their particular goals to the detriment of the community as a whole. Were the IAF organizations any different?

After listening and watching, I realize that what Cortes and Chambers are really talking about is a concept of self-interest based on both the physical and psychological needs for human growth. They focus on what people need to develop a sense of "self," essentially what people need to be human. And, of course, it begins with the basics for survival—food, shelter, and safety—which are often unmet needs among the people they seek to organize. Yet the IAF organizing approach recognizes the need for more than just the basics. To become fully human, people need skills for meaningful work. For self-respect, they need some control over their lives. For fulfillment, they need a sense of accomplishment. And for their own integrity, they need to feel that they matter, that their worth as human beings is recognized and that they have some visibility in the overall scheme of life, power, and politics. The development of self-interest, then, is a move not toward selfishness, but toward wholeness. It is a move toward harmonious living with others and competency in dealing with the complexities of life. It *is* indeed an internal revolution!

As I listen to Ed Chambers, Ernie Cortes, and Sister Christine Stephens, I begin to understand that the public actions of the IAF organizations and the manner in which they promote them are selected as much for how they provide for the self-interest and growth of individual men and women as for the importance of the issue itself. If the action that leads to a health clinic in a poor neighborhood provides opportunities for leadership, visibility, growth, affirmation, recognition, and respect for the neighborhood people who propose it, then it is worthwhile—a double hit: a service to keep people healthy and a process to learn how to be effective politically. But if Ernie Cortes, the community organizing expert, gets it for them in a closed-door meeting with a few politicians and city bureaucrats, the people affected don't learn that they are capable of acting for themselves. The Iron Rule has not been enforced. Cortes, the expert, acting alone, does nothing to develop the self-interest of the leaders who build and hold his organizations together. They become dependent on him every time they need something. When the time comes for him to leave, they would have neither the skills nor the insight to help themselves. So while it is often frustrating for a politician to meet with a dozen or so network leaders to discuss a zoning case or the intricacies of a state-federal matching formula for funding a water project, it is the way IAF leaders learn and develop a sense of their own worth.

"What we're trying to do is to allow people to become expert enough to challenge the experts," Cortes says.

This kind of approach over a long time can have a profound effect on the people who participate, particularly for people shut out of power because of their income, race, lack of education, or ignorance of social graces. It can change them, and through them, their families—perhaps even their neighborhoods and communities. But being able to make those deals depends on developing relationships with people who hold power, as well as with each other.

"We teach people that the relationship is more important than the issue," Cortes says. "If people's conception of self-interest is narrow, then it's okay to screw you if we're on different sides of the issue because we're enemies. But if we see the relationship as important, there is another dimension to it. Being right is not always as important as being reasonable. And being reasonable means that you review, look at your interests in a different way because of your relationship."

IAF leaders like Ed Chambers and Ernie Cortes believe that involvement with major political events can help develop both the spiritual and psychological integration of self—through a connection with other people and a mastery of skills and knowledge. But in their view, people can't do that until they come to terms with their own self-interest and their relationship with other people.

"For you to grow and develop, you have to get out of yourself into the skins of others," Cortes says. And in session after session, Cortes teaches hundreds of new political leaders in many states that every time they engage another individual on a deep level of human understanding, they also develop themselves spiritually and politically. He teaches these men and women that their leadership ability and recognition within the IAF organizations and the political arena as a whole depends not on protecting turf or holding power closely and wielding it arbitrarily, but on their ability to *expand* the numbers of their fellow leaders in the interest of the growth of the organization. Cortes promotes the one-on-one as the tool to do just that.

"It is the most radical thing we teach," he says.

Part Two

*Hope reminds us not to absolutize
the present, not to take it too seriously,
not to treat it too honorably,
because it will not last.*

Walter Brueggemann
Hope within History

8

The Black Hand
Over San Antonio

San Antonio, 1966

It is two weeks before the May Democratic Primary election. University of Texas graduate student Ernesto Cortes has recruited his aunts and neighbors to join him and other college students to stuff envelopes and go door-to-door for a Mexican-American attorney, John Alaniz, who is trying to get elected to the Bexar County Commissioners' Court, the official local government arm of the state of Texas. In San Antonio, the political heat is at the boiling point, particularly for those candidates like Alaniz who are backed by the emerging progressive coalition of Hispanics, blacks, teachers, unions, and limousine liberals who have won a few offices in the past but have never come close to seizing real power—a voting majority on any public body in the city or county. Now, with more than 100,000 of Bexar County's 235,000 registered voters living in the coalition's strongest voting precincts, the coalition is threatening to capture the majority vote on the five-member county commission and take over the local Democratic party organization. If Alaniz could win, he would join on the commission Albert Peña, who represents the West Side and who built a Hispanic political machine when he organized Viva Kennedy clubs in the 1960 presidential election. With Peña and Alaniz, plus the vote of the genial incumbent liberal County Judge Charles Grace, who is favored to defeat handily his election challenger, the coalition would control county government. Cortes and the young college-educated Hispanics coming of age in San Antonio and getting involved in politics for the first time are almost euphoric. Change is in the air. Particularly on the West Side, where most of the city's Hispanic population lives.

The West Side. Everyone knew it meant more than a designation or direction west of Interstate 10. It meant Mexicans—pure and simple. By the mid-1960s, Spanish was still the primary language of the West Side, which housed more than 200,000 people of Mexican heritage in small frame homes with pots of petunias in the yard and the stench of meat-packing plants in the air. On the West Side, people still paid the insurance man in weekly installments and placed flowers on the graves of loved ones on *Los Dias de Los Muertos*. They served tamales as Christmas treats and sat at the picnic tables on the corner at the convenience store, which sold single bottles of beer and homemade pastries. But many West Side residents had to send their children to schools that had no heat in winter. Families waged a continuing battle against rats that invaded their neighborhoods from the debris-filled drainage ditches that overflowed after a rain, sending rushes of water into the streets to flood homes, even to claim lives.

With Alaniz's candidacy and the growing strength of the new political "coalition," there is hope that the West Side is about to change. But in the final days of the campaign, San Antonio is agog over a television commercial showing a black hand hovering menacingly over the skyline of the city. An ominous voice booms forth: "The liberal element and militant minorities of our city are making a grandstand play to take over Bexar County. You cannot let this happen."[1]

In the key visual frame, political leader Peña is seen whispering into the ear of County Judge Grace, who puffs on a huge cigar. The implication is clear. Mexican Peña calls the shots. Grace is nothing more than a puppet. Add one more minority vote to the commission—Alaniz's—and you have a Mexican takeover. Danger and disaster lie ahead.

The same photograph with the same black hand over the city skyline is printed on 100,000 flyers that are mailed to voters in Anglo-dominated precincts. With the television attacks and the huge mail barrage, the campaign is shaping up to be the most costly—and controversial—in the county's history.

Supporters of Judge Grace, Peña, and Alaniz laugh it off. Who could fall for such blatant racism? Who could believe that Mexican hoards would take over and destroy the city? Or that Peña represented the forces of evil depicted in the political ads? Black hand, indeed!

But San Antonio voters do not laugh. They vote two-to-one to throw the good Judge Grace out of office. And they also defeat Alaniz and rout from office most of the candidates backed by the coalition. With the 1966 election, the black hand becomes an important symbol for San Antonio politics—a symbol of lingering racism and Hispanic frustration, of the power of organized money, and of the determination of the local bankers, lawyers, and old society families to keep the growing Mexican population from coming to power in San Antonio. By any means.

To understand what Ernesto Cortes and the Industrial Areas Foundation are doing in Texas and elsewhere in the nation, it helps to understand the black hand and San Antonio, Texas, a place *New Yorker* magazine writer Calvin Trillin once called the only city in Texas that anybody could accuse of being charming.[2] Trillin attributed that charm to San Antonio's sense of history and the dominating presence of its Spanish-speaking population. But neither were much valued by the German and Anglo merchants and landowners who controlled the city for almost 150 years. It was not without a struggle that the charming historic buildings, the scenic downtown river, and even the Alamo itself were preserved. And it was certainly not without turmoil that the city's "charming" Hispanic majority finally in the 1970s came into its own in this city of almost a million people.

Spanish explorers came to the San Antonio River and surrounding area in 1692, but the first permanent settlement, a missionary outpost, was not established until 1718, the year the French founded New Orleans. San Antonio's first settlers were Spanish subjects who had migrated to the Canary Islands before being sent to the new world by King Phillip V. By 1821 when Stephen F. Austin's first Anglo settlers arrived, San Antonio was the northern-most city of Mexico, its public life dominated by the descendants of the Canary Islanders, and its work carried out by poor Mexicans and Indians. The culture was old-world Catholic and overwhelmingly Hispanic. But Mexico could do nothing to stem the tide of European and American settlers that poured into the area, and, after Texas won its independence from Mexico in 1836, some of San Antonio's leading Hispanic citizens retreated into Mexico's interior. Most, however, pledged their loyalty to the new republic, only to find that their lives and culture soon began to undergo drastic changes. By 1850, five years after Texas joined the union, the city's institutions were in the hands of its French, German, and Anglo settlers, and by 1870, the Spanish-speaking were a minority. It made little difference that the Canary Islanders took great pains to distinguish themselves from the Mexicans. Virtually all Hispanics were soon shut out of the city's social and economic life. But that didn't stop a small, steady stream of immigrants from the south. San Antonio— only 200 miles from the Mexican border—was a powerful magnet for Mexico's dispossessed, particularly from 1910 to 1920 when turmoil surrounding the Mexican Revolution engulfed the region. The newcomers during this turbulent period included a few professional people, but most were poor peasants, fleeing the devastation of their homes and villages. Thousands of the new immigrants crowded into the flat, treeless western quadrant of San Antonio—the West Side—constituting a de facto segregated area, with all-Mexican neighborhoods, churches, and schools, and a culture and language separate from the city as a whole.

Because San Antonio's German and Anglo families had made their fortunes in cotton and cattle trading during the Civil War, they saw no reason to hustle for business development as did the more flamboyant and fast-moving entrepreneurs in Houston and Dallas. So in 1930 San Antonio lost its status as the largest city in Texas and remained a passive, sleepy town, its leading citizens satisfied to rest on old money and the trappings of high society at the top. But few groups have been less secure than San Antonio's old money, whose power was based on a cheap labor market and family connections—not necessarily on achievement or intellect.[3] The steady flow of Mexican immigrants provided the cheap labor for the city's menial jobs. But continued migration and high birth rates caused San Antonio's population growth to leap so far ahead of job growth that its Mexican West Siders slipped deeper into poverty. Only the presence of federal government military installations saved the city from the stifling atmosphere of a Banana Republic. With its five military bases and the resulting economic spillover, the federal government helped create a small middle class for San Antonio—providing almost one-third of all paying jobs in the city. Upwardly mobile Mexican-Americans dreamed of landing jobs at Kelly Air Force Base, which employed as many as 40,000 civilians and provided a decent living, as well as a measure of job security not subject to the vagaries of overt racial discrimination.

This was the San Antonio into which Ernesto Cortes, Jr. was born in 1943. Both his maternal and paternal grandparents had come to the city from Mexico during the revolution. One grandfather had been a Mexico City police official and the other had been a popular band leader. The Cortes family was hard working and solid as they sank their roots into San Antonio's Mexican-American community.

Cortes' father was manager of a Payless Drug Store until the early 1950s when he went to work for Pepsi Cola and traveled around South Texas. His mother stayed home to raise her three children: Ernie, his brother Ronnie, and a severely handicapped daughter, Yolanda, who was brain damaged at birth and who died when she was only 12 years old. Cortes recalls that his sister couldn't talk, walk, or sit up and had to be fed, held, and carried everywhere. Two years older than Ernie, she was cared for entirely by her mother, with help only from the Cortes extended family of aunts and uncles. There was no special medical treatment, no therapy, no community support groups. No hope.

"I had the unusual ability to get her to smile," Cortes recalls. "I was the only one. I can remember acting out and carrying on to get a little bit of a laugh that we could detect."

Like many families of children with disabilities, the Cortes family was sometimes subjected to stares, embarrassed silences, rude comments, and the kinds of disrespectful questions that create both stress and strength in a family. For Cortes, these memories will always be with him, a source of grief and anger.

"My mother told my wife that I once took in after some friends who made fun of my sister," Cortes says. "Now I guess I over-identify with people who are in this kind of situation."

Cortes' Catholic parents sent him to parochial schools, which provided a superior education to the underfunded public schools that dotted the West and South Sides of San Antonio. A chunky, intense little boy, Cortes memorized whole books and then wanted to talk about them. His teacher once sent him to the back of the room to read an encyclopedia so that he would stop disrupting her class by asking so many questions. Another teacher let him accumulate "indulgences" for reading the Bible 15 minutes a day—something Cortes did eagerly. "I loved the stories of David and Jonathan, Judas Maccabeus, Solomon, the adventure stories," he remembers.

But in spite of his Bible-reading, Cortes never wanted to be a priest. He recalls knowing too many boys who went into Catholic seminary at a young age and came out with horror stories about having to work too hard, get up too early in the morning, and spend too many hours on their knees praying. It was not a life that interested him—nor one his parents encouraged.

Although never really interested in politics, the Cortes family, like most of San Antonio's Hispanics, was delighted with the election to Congress of Henry B. Gonzalez in 1961. Gonzalez's election was significant in many ways. The first Hispanic elected to Congress from Texas, he was independent and honest and had risen to prominence in San Antonio without the assistance of the old families. His election for the first time demonstrated the potential clout of San Antonio's growing Hispanic population, which in the early 1960s only Gonzalez could fully arouse. His photograph adorned the walls of many Mexican-American homes, along with John F. Kennedy and the Virgin of Guadalupe. Once neighbors, the Cortes family took great pride in knowing Gonzalez personally, and Ernie's grandfather always placed a large election sign in his front yard every time Gonzalez was on the ballot. Even the old families came to tolerate Gonzalez, realizing the almost magical hold he had on West Side residents. It was better to leave him alone than to risk arousing the "sleeping giant," as the news media were beginning to describe the growing, but passive, Mexican-American population.

Cortes was close to his grandfather and his mother's brothers. Through his uncles, who stepped in to assist with family chores when Ernie's traveling father was on the road, Cortes made his first public-speaking appearances. One of his uncles entered Ernie, an eighth grader, in an Optimist Club public-speaking contest and took him to Optimist groups all over the city to make his speech. "It was a silly speech which I delivered eloquently, and my uncles thought the contest was rigged when I didn't win," he jokes.

At Central Catholic High School, Cortes continued his speech and debate activities and graduated when he was only 16 years old. He became the first member of his family to attend college when he went to Texas A&M University in the Fall of 1959. Although he laughs about it now, Cortes recalls the disappointed look on his assigned roommate's face when the boy realized he would be sharing a room for a whole year with a "greezer."

By the time Cortes was a college senior, he had decided that he didn't like the military atmosphere of Texas A&M, and he felt terribly depressed. "I was completing college in three years," he says. "I was tired, felt like I had wasted my time because I hadn't really learned anything. I didn't have any skills." During this period in his life, he was also beginning to be emotionally caught up in the turmoil of the civil rights movement. He, and countless other young Hispanics, saw parallels between their own experiences of discrimination and what was being reported from Birmingham or Selma on the evening news. Cortes' mind was also full of the heavy philosophical musings of Doestoevsky, Tolstoy, Faulkner, and T.S. Eliot. A basic skepticism was beginning to crowd his Catholic school-boy beliefs.

"I read all that stuff, remember lying in bed and not being able to sleep because of all the ideas. I vacillated between belief and disbelief," he says of this time, which he now understands to be more a "crisis of Catholicism" than a crisis of faith. His family shipped him off to relatives in Mexico City for a summer, where Cortes says he was "insufferable and obnoxious," demanding to know why his Mexican relatives did nothing to alleviate the poverty he saw in the capital. But in the fall, he entered graduate school at the University of Texas at Austin to study economics, and he became active in the University Y, an affiliate of the YMCA and a hotbed of student activism under the influence of the kinds of liberal Protestant ministers who brought their moral authority to bear on the Southern civil rights movement.

"It intrigued me that the cutting edge of the civil rights movement was with ministers. The churches themselves might be irrelevant, but there was an awful lot of religious ferment in the movement, and I intuitively felt that some kind of real inspiration was at work," he says.

Cortes' religious crisis receded and was replaced by a consuming interest in modern theology. One of his professors had suggested he read Reinhold Neibuhr's *The Nature and Destiny of Man,* and it was not long before Cortes was absorbing the ideas not only of Neibuhr, but of Tillich, Barth, and Bonhoefer. He considered entering seminary so that he could study theology in a more systematic way, and he even spent a few months working in a Beaumont church with a United Church of Christ pastor active in civil rights causes. But while immersing himself in Protestant theology, Cortes was also reintroduced to Catholicism.

"I got intrigued because people at the 'Y' knew more about Catholicism than I did, and they were non-Catholic, which meant that they had thought about it more than I," Cortes says. "Everyone was reading *The Secular City* by Harvey Cox. So did I. I started reading Neibuhr and Tillich and began getting more and more curious. I began reading the *Christian Century, Commentary,* and William Stringfellow." Cortes became convinced that his skepticism was not incompatible with his Catholicism nor with his growing need to act on his beliefs.

"Faith is important to me," he says. "The church—*churches*—are important to me. The Roman Catholic church, but also the concept of churches, the whole Judeo-Christian tradition, because I think there's mystery in life. There's awe. There are things beyond ourselves that we can't explain, no matter how smart we are."[4]

Like many bright young Mexican-Americans who were inspired by Martin Luther King, Jr., Cortes was soon captivated by the emergence of Cesar Chavez and his effort to organize farmworkers in California and Texas. Cortes felt that the deeply religious Chavez offered the same spiritual basis for political action as did King, and he hoped that it would lead to an awakening among Texas Hispanics. The "sleeping giant" was still slumbering away, unmindful of the power of its numbers and the potential for change. Chavez and his assistant Jim Drake, a former seminarian, were trying to organize farmworkers in the Rio Grande Valley, and Cortes helped by getting housewives to visit supermarket managers to enlist support for the boycott of melons, grapes, and lettuce. It was as much a social movement to liberate Hispanics as a union organizing effort. Even so, it was not enough for Cortes.

Little by little, Cortes also got sucked into San Antonio's electrifying local political wars, where a group of Hispanics, white liberals, blacks, and union members formed a rather disorganized coalition to challenge the Anglo business and professional establishment that ran the town and controlled city government. Some of the coalition-supported candidates managed to win a few races here and there, just enough to keep hope alive, but never enough to create any permanent power base. Every time the coalition threatened, something like the black hand would be used to scare away potential allies and voters.

Power in San Antonio in the mid-1960s was the sole domain of the nonpartisan Good Government League (GGL), composed of a group of socially prominent businessmen who had brought the council manager form of government to the city in 1951. By installing a government of experts and professionals, they hoped to rid San Antonio of the kinds of raucous, factionalized, and often corrupt politics that since the 1920s had embarrassed the prominent families who dominated the city's social and economic life. To ensure that assorted ruffians, Mexicans, and lower-class ward healers would never get the upper hand, Chamber of Commerce officials created the GGL in 1954 to handpick and supervise the election of trusted city council candidates. The GGL initially attracted as many as 3,000 business and civic leaders as active members, but the control and direction of the organization was closely held by a few dozen bankers, lawyers, retailers, and investors, either directly related to or acceptable to the old families. These GGL leaders feared controversy more than sin itself. So under their regime, politics gave way to administration. Good, gray, and stifling.

The organization's hold on San Antonio was so complete during its 18-year domination of city hall that only four of its 81 endorsed candidates failed to win election. Although the GGL's secret candidate selection committee put up a few token Mexican-Americans, as well as an occasional woman or black, almost 80 percent of the city's officeholders were Anglos who lived in northern San Antonio's most prosperous residential neighborhoods. With the defeat of the liberal coalition's candidates in the 1966 elections, GGL members extended their control to the county government and the city's legislative delegation to the state capital.

It was one thing to have pretty Mexican dancing girls grace the cover of Chamber of Commerce tourist brochures, but it was quite another to share power with the exploding Mexican-American population. As late as 1970, San Antonio's octogenarian mayor and GGL founder Walter W. McAllister appeared in an NBC-TV documentary saying that "our citizens of Mexican descent love beauty, flowers, music, dancing. But they're not quite, let's say, as ambitiously motivated as Anglos to get ahead financially. But they get a lot out of life."[5]

They may have gotten a lot out of life, but San Antonio's Mexican-Americans were certainly not getting much out of their city government. Under the GGL, the West Side consistently received lower levels of service than the Anglo North Side neighborhoods for such simple improvements as street pavings and repair work, drainage systems, public libraries, and new development.[6] But in the mid-1960s, there appeared to be little they could do about it.

GGL influence pervaded the city. The real decisions in city government on everything from electric rates to expressway routes were made, not in open council chambers, but in private meetings at the exclusive Argyle Club in suburban Alamo Heights or on the golf course at the San Antonio Country Club. Council members were elected city-wide instead of by geographic districts, driving up the cost of elections and increasing the importance of the well-financed, slate-card campaigns only the GGL could afford to run. The GGL had both money and moxie, as well as a willingness to manipulate Anglo voters' fears of a takeover by political radicals and militant Mexican-Americans.

It was a tough system to crack. But these were also the days of the Great Society, and federal money created other political opportunities for independent Hispanics—no matter how they were shunned by San Antonio's city government. Poverty warriors and liberal eastern philanthropic foundations developed a romance with *La Raza,* a term used by Hispanic militants to describe their common cultural and ethnic heritage. It was a rare Hispanic activist who could not find paid work to promote *la causa.* Ernie Cortes was no exception. By this time, he was married and the father of a baby girl, and he went to work for the Ford Foundation–funded Mexican American Unity Council, an innovative program that promoted private-public economic partnerships to bring Hispanics into the mainstream of business and financial activities.[7] There, he looked at economic development, job creation programs, and methods of organizing working poor people to act in their economic interests.

But by the early 1970s, the promise of the Great Society had fizzled. Richard Nixon was president. The Democratic party was in disarray. More than 10 years of intensive political activity among independent Hispanics in San Antonio had gotten nowhere. The Mexican American Unity Council was running restaurants, and the United Farm Workers Union was on the verge of becoming a nostalgic memory in Texas. The GGL was still firmly in control of city and county politics, and Mexicans in San Antonio were still shut out of power and locked in poverty. The old ways didn't work, and it was time to face it, Cortes thought.

The 1970 census showed that for the first time since the Civil War, Hispanics constituted a majority of the population of San Antonio. But Cortes believed it would be a majority without power or influence or even hope unless someone found a way to awaken the "sleeping giant" and mobilize it to act in its own self-interest. If such a way existed, Ernie Cortes decided he would find it.

In the summer of 1971, Cortes went to Chicago to meet Ed Chambers and to check out the Industrial Areas Foundation, founded by the colorful and outrageous patron saint of community organizing in America, Saul Alinsky. Cortes had met Alinsky once at the University of Texas during a speaking engagement and had found him somewhat arrogant and egotistical. But Cortes believed that Alinsky's training had made a first-rate organizer out of Cesar Chavez, who worked for him after World War II. Maybe there was something Cortes, too, could learn.

9

Tactics Is the Art of Taking

Chicago, 1964

Mayor Richard Daley of Chicago has pulled out all the stops to turn out a huge Democratic vote for Lyndon Johnson against Barry Goldwater in the November presidential election. He has lined up most of the city's black organizations to cooperate in the Democratic get-out-the-vote effort. But only six weeks before the election, leaders of the black Woodlawn Organization regret acting so hastily—not because of anything Johnson or the national Democrats had done, but because their too-early presidential endorsement seems to endanger their own local political goals.

With the help of Saul Alinsky in 1960, The Woodlawn Organization (TWO) had been organized by a group of black residents and church leaders to keep the University of Chicago from expanding into their neighborhoods. After its successful effort against the university, the group decided to focus on other projects to upgrade their community, and TWO had become a force to be reckoned with in Chicago politics. This year, the city administration had committed to make certain capital improvements in TWO neighborhoods. But with the virtual lockup of the black vote for the Democrats, Mayor Daley and city officials were under very little pressure to deliver on their commitments to TWO—at least for now. What's the hurry?

But TWO members *are* in a hurry, and when they realize they have given away their leverage to get the city to focus on the neighborhoods, they decide they have to do something drastic to get the mayor's attention.

O'Hare Airport—the world's busiest airport and Chicago's pride—becomes their target. Thousands of travelers pass through its gates each day, and most of them stop long enough to use the bathroom facilities. TWO decides to occupy the lavatories—a sure way to bring airport operations to a halt! All demonstrators have to do is drop a dime, enter the restroom stall, and push the lock on the door. It would take only a few people, armed with books and newspapers, staying there all day to disrupt the airport and create chaos. There might even be fist fights in the long lines when travelers realize they are about to miss their connections and have no place to relieve themselves. Angry passengers would no doubt shout at airport employees. Children would be screaming, "But I've got to go!" And what could the Chicago police do about it? Break into restroom stalls and demand evidence of legitimate occupancy? O'Hare would soon become a shambles. Planes might even have to be held up so passengers could reboard to use the toilet facilities. The scene could become a source of acute embarrassment to Mayor Daley and the city administration, which prides itself on running a city that "works." TWO members laugh when they think of the chaotic scenes that would be flashed on television newscasts all over the country—and, of course, they would make sure the TV cameras would be on location to record every detail. It would be great fun, and it would certainly get the mayor's attention in this critical election season.

TWO leaks word of its plans to city administrators, and within 48 hours TWO leaders are meeting with city officials who say they have always intended to live up to their commitments, and how could anyone get the idea that a promise made by city hall would not be kept? TWO gets what it wants from the city, and the O'Hare toilet tie-up never occurs.

TWO members learn two important rules of political action from this experience: First, people in power can usually absorb all kinds of verbal brickbats, but they never want to be laughed at or ridiculed. And second, the threat of action is sometimes more terrifying than the action itself.[1]

Those rules and dozens of others, were laid down over a 30-year career of controversy by the community organizer Saul Alinsky.

Alinsky was an original political thinker and a classic American entrepreneur. If he had turned his talents to business, he would have been in a league with Stephen Jobs—the Apple computer wizard who was loaded with ideas and capable of making a fortune and changing an industry, but who had to be eased out of his own company when the investors tired of flamboyance and demanded attention to detail and profits.

Alinsky's business was organizing people—more than two million in his lifetime.[2] But he was never eased out of anything. It was not the nature of community organizations to focus on the bottom line. And because most of the organizations Alinsky worked with were composed of poor people living in poor neighborhoods, the successes he brought them—even if they were short-lived—were like manna from heaven. Who would dare demand anything more? Besides, Alinsky generated excitement, controversy, and a frenzy of activity wherever he went. Once in the early 1940s when he tried to organize in Kansas City, the police chief met him at the train station and immediately locked him up.[3] At various times he was called a troublemaker, an outside agitator, a cynic, a conservative, a radical, an atheist, a tool of the Catholic church—even a Communist, the only label that had no basis in fact. But the labels and his famous confrontational tactics caused business and civic leaders to huddle in nervous anticipation of what he might do in their communities. Newspaper editorials sometimes lauded his goals but always decried his tactics. Yet poor people walked a little taller after one of his actions, and several generations of community activists memorized his words. Despite the fear and adulation, however, Alinsky was never able to realize his own goal of building regional or national networks of community power organizations or of training more than a few first-rate organizers. His organizations died when the issues faded, the controversy cooled, the press lost interest, or when he, himself, moved on.

Building a broad-based power organization requires daily attention to detail. Former Industrial Areas Foundation organizer and journalist Nicholas Von Hoffman describes it as "the tedious job of stringing beads on a necklace."[4] Alinsky was too impatient to string beads. But his specific legacy, the Industrial Areas Foundation, is described by former San Antonio Mayor Henry Cisneros as the largest and most powerful community organizing effort in the United States.[5] Alinsky's general legacy of ideas and tactics helped fuel the civil rights movement, the community action programs of the War on Poverty, welfare rights organizations, and the burgeoning neighborhood association activism in the 1970s and 1980s. No doubt about it, Alinsky was an innovator. But in the late 1930s when this son of Russian Jewish immigrants was starting out, all he had was a way with words and a few big ideas.

Fresh out of the University of Chicago with a degree in sociology, Alinsky landed a job with the Institute for Juvenile Research to look at causes of juvenile crime in a poor area of Chicago. It was known as Back of the Yards because of its proximity to the stock yards. But Alinsky was an activist, not an academic, and he began to help John L. Lewis' newly formed CIO organize the meat-packing workers. He discovered that he could persuade people to move, to act, and to make things happen. Although he soon dropped research as a career, Alinsky was not cut out to be a union organizer either. He was more interested in finding ways to improve the lives of workers *outside* the plants rather than inside. He wanted to organize the communities where they lived.

Because Chicago's Catholic Bishop Bernard Sheil had supported the CIO organizing effort, Alinsky brought the bishop his ideas about organizing people who lived in urban industrial areas. Urban community organizing had started with Jane Addams' Hull House in Chicago in 1890, the same year the western frontier closed. But it remained essentially a settlement house movement to relieve the symptoms of poverty and urban pressures among the rural poor and foreign immigrants who were crowding into America's cities, which by 1920 had become home to half of all Americans. Alinsky outlined a bold new approach to deal with the problems of the urban poor, and Bishop Sheil was intrigued by the possibilities. He urged Alinsky to proceed by setting up a nonprofit foundation, to which he pledged his help.

Together, the bishop and Alinsky got Marshall Field III, heir to the multimillion-dollar department store fortune, to put money into the project. By 1940, Alinsky and Bishop Sheil had formally organized the Industrial Areas Foundation. It's purpose was "to restore the democratic way of life to modern industrial society."[6]

Alinsky's basic philosophy came directly from Thomas Jefferson's concept of neighborhood wards—small groups of people who could meet regularly to work out everyday community problems. But Alinsky wanted these local units to be run by neighbors and citizens rather than by professional politicians or bureaucrats. To Alinsky, the key was the right of people to form voluntary associations—to speak out on public issues and to protest actions of government when they appeared to be wrong.

Never seriously attracted to Marxist ideology, Alinsky fervently believed in democracy—the ability of people to decide for themselves. He was committed to decentralization, equality before the law, and freedom from want. Alinsky considered himself a radical in the best American tradition, and his desire to return to the principles of Madison, Jefferson, and Paine was the basis for his claim to radicalism, which by definition means getting back to origins or roots. His view of the historic struggle for power among American liberals, conservatives, and radicals led him to believe that the most fundamental meaning of what it meant to be American centered around a feeling for people.

> There were and are a number of Americans—few, to be sure—filled with deep feeling for people. They know that people are the stuff that makes up the dream of democracy. These few were and are the American radicals and the only way that we can understand the American radical is to understand what we mean by this feeling for and with people. Psychiatrists, psychologists, sociologists, and other learned students call this feeling "identification" and have elaborate and complicated explanations about what it means. For our purposes it boils down to the simple question, How do you feel about people?[7]

For Alinsky, again drawing on Jefferson, there were only two ways to feel about people: You could fear and distrust them, take away their power and give it to an elite, educated class; or you could identify with people, cherish and invest in them, and have confidence in their ability to shape their own lives. Like Jefferson, Alinsky chose to believe in people because for him, it was simply the most practical way to operate. He believed that self-interest, rather than idealism, influenced motivations and actions. So he appealed to the self-interest of the people he organized, as well as to the people he challenged. He divided people into three classes: the "Haves," the "Have-Nots," and the "Have-a-Little, Want Mores." And he forcefully laid out the proposition that it was in the self-interest of the "Haves" to give up some of their power and wealth to the "Have-Nots," who would try to get it anyway because it was in *their* self-interest to survive.

> I believe that man is about to learn that the most practical life is the moral life and that the moral life is the only road to survival. He is beginning to learn that he will either share part of his material wealth or lose all of it. . . . The fact is that it is not man's better nature but his self-interest that demands that he be his brother's keeper. We now live in a world where no man can have a loaf of bread while his neighbor has none. If he does not share his bread, he dare not sleep, for his neighbor will kill him. To eat and sleep in safety man must do the right thing, if for seemingly the wrong reasons, and be in practice his brother's keeper.[8]

Alinsky also developed his philosophy of organizing from two other American experiences: the trade union movement and agrarian populism.[9] From the Labor movement, he developed the idea that he must work within—and not try to overthrow—the existing economic system. The only way to do that was to develop a countervailing power to economic power. He believed that poor people could control their lives when they joined with others to confront the politicians and corporations that had the power to force change. Individuals would never have a chance acting alone; only organized people could balance organized money.

From the Populist movement, Alinsky learned to articulate his permanent bias for the people without power or influence who are "chained together by the common misery of poverty, rotten housing, disease, ignorance, political impotence, and despair."[10] He also learned to value the "bottom up" method of running organizations, where members, not just self-appointed leaders, made the decisions that affected their lives.

Despite his self-proclaimed radicalism, these beliefs grew out of traditions as American as apple pie. Alinsky simply wanted to make the system work, and he believed he could do so by organizing to empower people.

Alinsky's first success came in his hometown of Chicago—at about the same time the IAF itself came into being. The first convention of the Back of the Yards Organization in 1939 focused on the issues of "disease, dirt, deterioration, dependence and delinquency." Thousands of people turned out for this and other meetings at which Alinsky crowded hundreds of people into the offices of bureaucrats or staged demonstrations through residential neighborhoods where city officials lived. Many confrontations and several months later, Back of the Yards claimed credit for new police patrols, street repairs, regular garbage collection, and lunch programs for 1,400 children.

By 1940, Alinsky was receiving requests from other cities for his organizing services. He quickly put together organizations in Kansas City and St. Paul. But neither was as successful as Chicago, primarily because Alinsky spent little time with them. He had no structure or support staff to nurture his urban neighborhood organizations. Then World War II intervened, and Alinsky, at the urging of friends, put his thoughts into a book that became the Bible of community organizing—*Reveille for Radicals*, published in 1945. It was a witty, concise statement that ripped apart organized labor, liberal do-gooders, indifferent bureaucrats and public officials, dinosaur corporations, and sentimental efforts at public charity. It also laid out a blueprint for developing power organizations among poor people in urban neighborhoods. The success of the book, as well as Alinsky's showmanship, created great demand for his services. Appeals for his help came from California, St. Louis, New York City, Montana, and communities all over the country. So Alinsky began to hire other organizers to develop the local organizations.

Two of his early organizers were Fred Ross and Cesar

Chavez, who, under Ross' direction in the late 1940s, formed the Community Service Organization (CSO) to reach Hispanics in the Southwest. Under Ross' leadership, CSO expanded to 30 chapters in California and Arizona. But Alinsky's first wife died in 1947, and his subsequent depression and withdrawal from organizing work for a brief period left Ross on his own. By the late 1950s, CSO had split from the IAF, and by 1962, Cesar Chavez had formed his own United Farm Workers Union. When Alinsky returned to full-time organizing in 1951, he began trying to create a national network of organizations under the IAF banner.

The patterns of organizing developed in Back of the Yards and other early organizations became the blueprint for all of IAF's later organizing efforts. Local church and community leaders would invite Alinsky into their cities to form an organization to tackle community problems long ignored or about to explode. Under Alinsky's guidance, the local organization would determine who had the power to solve the problem. Then they would begin organizing people to stage a dramatic public confrontation against a recognizable enemy—the president of the utility company or the banker who handled the city's finances. The glare of public attention and pressure usually precipitated a crisis so uncomfortable that public officials or business leaders had little choice but to begin negotiations with the local organizations. When everything came off as planned and the organization won some of its demands, Alinsky would leave town and the local people carried on as best they could.

Churches in urban areas became the backbone of these early organizing efforts, particularly the Catholic church. Bishop Sheil's early support opened the doors to Catholic money and involvement. But one of Alinsky's greatest allies in the Catholic church was Irish-American Monsignor John O'Grady. O'Grady had organized and become the director of the National Conference of Catholic Charities in the 1920s, and he had a string of contacts within the church that Alinsky was able to weave into an effective social action network. After World War II, O'Grady felt that Alinsky could help Catholic Charities put their attention back into the streets of urban neighborhoods. He thought community organizing could provide the environment for urban churches to survive.[11]

Although Alinsky's closeness to the Catholic church sometimes caused concern among urban Protestants, many actively supported the IAF organizations with money and members. In fact, a group of Protestant ministers in the 1960s developed a statement that outlined a theological basis for Protestant involvement with Alinsky's organizing. It centered around the Christian approach to fulfill Jesus' mission to the powerless, the poor, and the racially segregated.[12]

Alinsky himself was not religious—in fact, he was skeptical about organized religion. But he believed that his organizations needed to have some institutional base, some source of strength and support capable of withstanding the pressures that would be brought on poor people when the going got tough. The churches were among the few institutions that remained voluntarily in those poor neighborhoods, already organized and providing people with at least some understanding of the dynamics of group participation. Because Alinsky believed that all organizing was reorganizing, it was an alliance of practicality—on Alinsky's part at least, and for the churches as well because Alinsky provided one of the few concrete methods for their poor parishioners to get some actual assistance.

Father John Egan, a Chicago priest who became an IAF booster, said he was attracted to Alinsky because he "wanted to do for people what I believed God wanted done—to give them freedom and some say over the things that affected them."[13] But when friends like Father Egan suggested that there be more discussion of religious values within the organizations, Alinsky dismissed the idea, saying "you take care of the religion, Jack, we'll do the organizing."[14]

For Alinsky, confrontation and controversy were essential to organizing, and if the tactics he used made his church allies uncomfortable, that was just too bad. Alinsky taught them that "change means movement. Movement means friction. Only in the frictionless vacuum of a nonexistent abstract world can movement or change occur without that abrasive friction of conflict."[15] If priests and ministers wanted to improve the lives of their church members, Alinsky believed they would just have to learn to fight. "In the world of give-and-take," he wrote, "tactics is the art of how to take and how to give. Here our concern is with the tactic of taking: how the Have-Nots can take power away from the Haves."[16]

He believed an enemy had to be clearly identified for confrontational tactics to succeed, because the major purpose of all of his tactics was to maintain constant pressure on the opposition.

"Pick the target, freeze it, personalize it and polarize it."

"Ridicule is man's most potent weapon."

"Power is not only what you have but what the enemy thinks you have."

"A good tactic is one that your people enjoy."

"The threat is usually more terrifying than the thing itself."[17]

Operating under these rules—which often produced dramatic media events—Alinsky was aggressive, relentless, imaginative, humorous, and outrageous. When he was engaged in a battle against Kodak in Rochester, New York, in the mid-1960s, Alinsky, in something of a self-parody of his own tactics, threatened to buy 100 tickets to one of Rochester's symphony concerts and feed the predominantly black members of the local organization a dinner of baked beans a few hours before they went to the concert. The resulting "stink-in" would be a surefire attention getter. The threat met his criteria for an effective tactic: It would be unexpected, and it would expose Rochester's elite and their pretensions to culture to ridicule. There was no law against it. It might be fun. And it would probably get action quickly because the social elite wouldn't want "those people" to invade their activities again.

By the early 1960s, Alinsky had trained almost a dozen organizers on projects in more than a dozen major cities. But he couldn't hold on to them. Organizers burned out or became disillusioned with the hectic lives they were required to live: always on the road, constantly overworked, underpaid, under siege, and most importantly, operating with little or no direction from Alinsky, who acted as a Lone Ranger whenever it suited his mood. For the organizers, it was always start and start over. Very few organizations survived when the organizers left town for a new venture.

In 1965, when he was invited into Rochester, New York, after serious street clashes between blacks and police, the only experienced organizers left in the IAF were Ed Chambers and Richard Harmon. Alinsky was 56 years old and had become the guru of organizing in the United States. But he was tired, and so it was Chambers, a former Benedictine seminarian from

Iowa and the current director of the IAF, whom Alinsky sent to Rochester. And it was Chambers who did the gritty work of organizing while Alinsky breezed into town periodically to advise on strategy and talk with the press. Alinsky spent less time organizing and more time becoming a celebrity—a talker rather than a doer.

"He was gravitating to activity and movement-style politics, traveling from campus to campus giving lectures and canned speeches. The kids loved him. But he was losing patience with the tediousness of the process," according to Chambers.

The tedious process of organizing in Rochester continued— without Alinsky's attention or full-time help. Nevertheless, it resulted in one of the most celebrated struggles in IAF history.

Attracting national news attention because of media focus on civil rights issues, the local IAF organization became embroiled in a major battle over jobs for blacks at the huge Kodak plant. Kodak had 41,000 employees in Rochester, and FIGHT, the Alinsky-affiliated organization, wanted job training for 600 blacks.[18] FIGHT had forged a similar agreement with Xerox, another of Rochester's major employers. But Kodak balked, first signing agreements, then reneging on them and resorting to heavy-handed tactics designed to run Alinsky's organization out of town. In the process, Kodak became the kind of enemy the IAF loved to hate. FIGHT staged daily demonstrations, organized a stock proxy battle, enlisted the assistance of Catholic Bishop Fulton J. Sheen, generated national TV coverage, and used the constant pressure of typical Alinsky tactics to goad Kodak into overreacting and hurting itself with its own superior strength. When Alinsky's house was broken into and Kodak sympathizers were widely suspected of having something to do with it, FIGHT knew that it had finally baited the giant corporation into reacting in a way that damaged its credibility and embarrassed it before its clients and customers. Public opinion was so mobilized against Kodak by this time that it had little option other than to reach a settlement with FIGHT on job training programs.

Although the IAF achieved what it wanted—a summer without race riots, the movement of blacks into the employment ranks of Rochester's major corporations, and the recognition that FIGHT was a black power organization to be reckoned with—the battle took its toll on the IAF. Rochester was to be its last public victory of the decade.

"I was organizing Rochester, supervising The Woodlawn Organization in Chicago, taking care of a project in Kansas, supervising Harmon in Buffalo. I just couldn't do it," Chambers said. "And Saul wasn't doing any organizing. There had to be a better way. We had to attract more people to organizing."

Chambers decided that he, too, would leave organizing unless the IAF found a way to do things differently. "We had to come up with a way to train and develop people systematically. We always sacrificed the training of people for the actions. We did actions as well as anybody. We won. We had a reputation. But where were the kinds of organizers and leaders who grew and developed instead of sitting on their organizations for years?" Chambers said.

Even in the IAF's home base of Chicago, now without the constant attention of an IAF organizer, the black leadership in TWO was keeping all the power for themselves. There was no expansion of leadership, no understanding of the purposes of holding power, no inclusion of other people, no growth, no development. What was going wrong?

"It hit me in FIGHT," Chambers said. "I wanted our primary purpose to be a commitment to the training and development of organizers, not to activity. That's when I told Saul it was my last project. I was coming back to Chicago to train organizers."

Alinsky was jolted by his lead organizer's determination. "Who's going to pay you to do this?" he asked Chambers.

"You are," Chambers told him. "You've got to raise the money."

And that is just what Alinsky did. For he, too, had been bothered by the lack of trained organizers and the absence of the political development of the people he organized. Back in the early 1950s, he had even sought funding from a dozen foundations to support the hiring and training of organizers to set up volunteer community organizations. But he got little response and dropped the idea. The only training his organizers received was on the job, plus a few hours now and then of free-wheeling, no-holds-barred discussions with Alinsky, lasting late into the night and fueled by good whiskey. Alinsky's biographer David Finks says it was "all done with wit and Alinsky's brand of rough, Socratic give and take."[19]

But it was not enough. Alinsky realized that he had better find a way to "construct" the experience of organizing for his students. "Most people go through life undergoing a series of happenings, which pass through their systems undigested," Alinsky said. "Happenings become experiences when they are reflected on, related to general problems, and synthesized. . . . Our job was to shovel those happenings back into the student's system so he could digest them into experience."[20]

With $200,000 from Gordon Sherman of the Midas International Company and $200,000 from the Rockefeller Foundation for the first scholarships, the IAF Training Institute opened in 1969. Chambers was its director and Dick Harmon its assistant director. The original plan was for 40 potential organizers to enroll in a 15-month training course that included lectures by Alinsky and practical training in projects to be set up in the Chicago area.

It was Chambers, rather than Alinsky, however, who began to figure out how to construct those experiences that would reach potential organizers on an emotional level to give them some direct understanding and to enable them to learn. It was a process of trial and error, hit and miss.

"Part of the challenge to me was that I knew this stuff so well, had it so deep in my gut, that I ought to be able to teach it. But could I get up in front of people and communicate and teach the experience I'd had and digested? I began by just trying things out," Chambers said.

Alinsky would come into the training session and spend about two hours, cover the same thing he covered the time before, and move on. He was bored with the training institute and began to develop a different kind of organization in the early 1970s. He was convinced that the middle class could come to understand the source of their problems, what he believed to be the out-of-control corporations that manipulated their lives through advertising and induced consumer buying binges. He sought to reach people across "older antagonisms" by bringing together the poor and middle class, professionals and blue-collar workers, ethnics and blacks around issues such as utility rates and pollution from steel mills.[21] But like most community-action organizations of the 1960s and early 1970s, his new group did not reach deeply enough into the center of the experiences of its members to make any lasting effect on them. It sought to attract people to issues, rather than to values or the roots of their public and private beliefs. As a result, it also began to falter—as did the aging Alinsky's attention and energy. It was to be his last effort.

10

When People Act
on the Gospel Values

Chicago, 1971

When Ernie Cortes came to the Industrial Areas Foundation Training Institute in 1971, Saul Alinsky was conspicuous by his absence. Edward Chambers was fully in charge, struggling to build a program to attract and train professional organizers. When Alinsky died of a heart attack in 1972, it was Chambers who had to scramble to raise money to keep the training institute alive. Alinsky's speaking fees had supplemented foundation grants to underwrite the program, and now without Alinsky, it was going to be difficult for the IAF to survive financially.

"The first five years I had to sell my soul to raise money. Foundations wouldn't fund us and I had to figure out a way to make it self-sufficient," Chambers recalls.

Everything was in a state of flux within the IAF—the money, the ties with local organizations, the concept of organizing, and the development of training programs for organizers and volunteer leaders. Then Ernie Cortes came along and dropped into the brewing stew his interest in theological concerns.

At first, Chambers resisted incorporating religious and theological reflection in the IAF's training process. After all, he was a tough, street-fighting organizer with a streak of skepticism stiffening his spine. He had trained with rough-talking Alinsky and had served under him for 15 years. Besides, Chambers had once been seared for his religious beliefs when, as a young Benedictine seminarian, he had questioned the practices of the Catholic church in the days before Vatican II. When he threw his existential beliefs at the rigidly organized precepts of church orthodoxy, he was asked to leave the seminary. He was only 23 years old at the time and went from there to Dorothy Day's Catholic Worker movement in New York. But his idealism in serving the poor eventually led to the deterioration of his health—he was even too weak to make a blood donation. He also felt useless because his sacrifices made no lasting changes in people's lives.

"Chambers saw the danger of mixing religious teachings with organizing because they have a tendency to deteriorate into sentimentality," Cortes says. "Chambers was afraid it was too soft."

Ed Chambers was not a soft man. In his early 40s when he found himself trying to hold the IAF together, Chambers assumed an air of authority few seriously questioned. Sister Maribeth Larkin, an IAF organizer, says the first time she was around Chambers he "scared the hell out of me. In the early days when he'd shout or use profanities, he would really shock me."[1]

Chambers delighted in shocking and in testing his organizers to the limit, and Ernie Cortes was no exception. Chambers challenged him relentlessly. How could Cortes' religious feeling possibly be integrated into the organizing process? How could he keep it from being phony, or worse, hypocritical? How could there be any toughness to this stuff? How would it correspond to people's lives here and now?

"Ed's initial reaction to things is always 'that's crazy,'" Cortes says. "But that's okay because it forces you to think through what you want to do."

Although Chambers was skeptical, the wide-ranging theological discussions continued among the staff and lead organizers. "Chambers and Harmon had a philosophy, almost a theology of organizing, although that was not what they called it," Cortes says. "What impressed me was that they had read a lot of the same books I had and they had thought about some questions I was really wrestling with. Like what is this business of organizing all about? What is its connection to public life generally? How does it relate to people's growth?"

Cortes says the atmosphere in Chicago was more helpful to him than he ever could have imagined. "I began to get some insight into myself and the whole process of organizing," he says. "What Chambers taught was a systematic way to organize—not just an emotional wave. I came to see that organizing was not just action and issues, but also values and vision."

The challenges from Chambers, the discussions with Harmon, the reading and reflection at last gave Cortes the opportunity to integrate his scholarly inclinations and interest in theology with some practical grass-roots organizing. The IAF Training Institute—not merely books and talk—provided hands-on experience through the development of several community organizations in the Chicago area. Although Alinsky's works, *Reveille for Radicals* and *Rules for Radicals*, were nominal "textbooks," the real teachers were experience and reflection—learning what worked in the real world and taking the time to find out why.

A significant feature for Cortes was the development of a vision for the kind of people's organization that he and others in the IAF wanted to build. What should it *be?* Where should it *lead?* What were you organizing *for?* What did you want people to *learn?*

To come up with answers, Chambers, Harmon, Cortes, and others began a serious analysis of the successes and failures in not only the IAF's history of community organizing, but within the 1960s civil rights and antiwar movements, and within a whole range of civic and service organizations that attracted the kinds of people they wanted to organize. They discovered several striking patterns common to most volunteer citizen's organizations—patterns that created instability, ineffectiveness, and eventual dissolution:

—*Movements that depended on charismatic leaders fell apart in the absence of the leader.*

—*Organizations formed around a single issue died when the issue lost its potency.*

—*Organizations that relied on public money, private grants, or the largess of a few wealthy contributors could never become truly independent.*

—Organizations that became overly procedural lost the momentum and flexibility to act.

—Organizations whose leaders acted autonomously without a system of internal accountability became corrupt when no one monitored their actions.

—Organizations that played to the public spotlight confused their desire for media attention with their strategy for change.

—Organizations that scrambled continuously to respond to a crisis got caught up in a whirlwind of activity that soon exhausted their leaders.

But the most important critique of movements and community organizations centered around the fact that once an organization folded, people were as powerless as they had always been—even after solving a specific problem or enacting a particular law. The power to regularly shape decisions that affected their lives was still not within the grasp of most middle-class and working poor people. If IAF organizations and IAF-trained organizers were to be effective, they would have to grapple with the fundamental issue of political power. That meant asking some essential questions about building a political organization: What if your organization's purposes were broader than solving single problems? What if your purpose was to amass power that would allow action on a wide range of issues? What if you sought the kind of power that lifted you to a different level of political decision-making? What if you could become a frequent player in the crafting of public policy? What if you had an organization that could survive not only its defeats on single issues, but its victories as well?

More questions and conversation: What if you began to appeal to people not on specific issues, but on something they valued? On something that was intrinsically important to them and for which they were willing to sacrifice? What if your organization could enhance what people valued? Would they then be willing to make a permanent commitment to an organization that seemed to care for them and operate with them on a deep level of fundamental concern? Would you be able to count on the longevity of the organization—no matter what happened to individual leaders or specific causes?

Within the IAF in the early 1970s, answers to these questions began to take shape, and the concept of seeking broad power and building organizations around values began to provide a central organizing strategy. This new direction meshed with the personal experiences of both Cortes and Chambers.

For Cortes, his Mexican roots helped shape his views that values mattered more than issues. For example, the people Cortes wanted to organize on the South and West Sides of San Antonio cared about "family." Family was a supreme value in their lives. And family, for most of the Hispanic working poor, was also intertwined with feelings for church. When you value something, you are willing to make a sacrifice for it; there is a cost you are willing to pay. Cortes knew that Mexican parents willingly sacrificed for their children—and often for their church. By talking about family values, could you motivate and organize people to act politically in their own genuine self-interest?

Talking about the positive value of families would be a radical departure from the movement rhetoric of the 1960s and early 1970s. Yet Ed Chambers sensed that poor people might be hungry for it. "The movements [of the 1960s] never attracted the moderate and conservative sections of the country," he wrote.[2] The majority of Americans, he felt, thought that movement people were "willing to trample on traditions for a single cause." But old movement images and language would not suffice for the strains and stresses of the 1970s and 1980s, Chambers argued. The new organizations had to reach into the heart. They had to connect with people at a core level of essential value. The idea of protecting and enhancing families might make that possible.

Cortes agreed, adding an important caveat. "You can't just be romantic about families," he says. "Unrealistic romantic notions about family can lead to fascism. Families can turn out to be oppressive. But families and traditions are useful and important, and you always have to see them in relation to other things. It is the give-and-take of family life, in the sacrifices and compromises that you make for the family that you learn to be human. It is where you learn to nurture and be nurtured."

For Chambers, the concept of family also struck a resonant—and personal—note. Giving up the life of a professional bachelor, he got married in his mid-40s and began having children at the same time as he was struggling to transform the IAF.

Family mattered to him now in a way that he had never before experienced, and he began to understand the pressures working families felt to stay intact and to keep children safe from harm. Particularly in poor urban communities. Families were under siege—affected by the corrosive effects of alcohol and drug abuse, crime, and the physical deterioration of neighborhoods. But the pressures were economic, too.

"The American family has become a money machine," Chambers wrote. "Month after month it must meet the food bills, mortgage or rent, car and other transportation costs, insurance premiums, non-insured health items, clothing costs, taxes, utilities and fuel, school expenses. . . . Both parents must work to fuel the family money machine, to meet the basic cost of keeping the family alive. Too often, what they work so hard for is undone by their own hard work . . . they have no energy left for the love and care of their children."[3]

If you began to talk to people about their families—and about how they might protect and help them by becoming involved in community organizations—and if you talked about their own individual growth and development in the process, then you might have a strategy that could lead to stable political organizations anchored by people whose values derived from concerns deeper than transitory issues. "In organizations based on values, social change is not some kind of abstraction that happens out there," Chambers also wrote. "It happens to people. It involves your whole life."[4]

As the IAF began to clarify its vision of community-based power organizations centered around values, its language also began to change. "I'd had a little training in philosophy," Chambers says. "And I started forcing myself to look at what our kind of organizing meant to people. We worked with people in the churches, and their language was the language of the gospel. Their language was nothing like Alinsky's language. His language was power talk. Tough, abrasive, confrontational, full of ridicule. And those are really all non-Christian concepts. So I started looking at it. Here are the non-Christian concepts . . . here are the Christian concepts. Are there any similarities? Is this just a different language for the same thing?"

Because he was now bringing lay church people from urban neighborhoods into the training sessions as well as organizers, synthesizing power talk with church talk became very important to Chambers. And he began to see some exciting possibilities. "When people act on the gospel values and hold one another accountable, you've got a revolutionary act," he discovered.

As Chambers worked on ways to assist in the development of leaders and minimize their dependence on the IAF organizer for ideas and leadership, he realized that organizers had to become teachers. And that meant they had to become readers and thinkers, as well as doers. If organizers were going to teach leaders about power and talk with them about values, they had to have an understanding of what was happening in the world around them—from the effects of television on people's lives to the roles of mediating institutions[5] in a democracy to the dynamics of the market system. That meant they had to know who held vast economic power—not only at the local level, but nationally and internationally as well. How were major U.S. corporations linked to law firms, the media, the politicians, even the church? What were people really up against when they challenged entrenched economic power? Or when their values conflicted with the overriding value of the modern market economy—money. More importantly, the IAF organizers and leaders had to understand the effects of public-sector decisions on private lives. They had to know the philosophy of modern corporate management, the dynamics of political decision-making, and the effects of concentrated economic power on the political process, and on and on.

So it was not just tactics—how to confront an enemy, stage a demonstration, hold a politician accountable, get out the vote, develop an issue, lobby a legislator, or get publicity—that characterized the IAF's evolving training program. Those elements were, of course, part of the training that organizers and leaders experienced. But there was more. The IAF kept breaking new ground, taking new risks, and moving into areas that most community organizers avoided.

In the years of experimentation, Chambers discovered one other crucial factor in the growth and development of the people he wanted to organize: the power of relationships. It is what he calls "mentoring and tutoring." It is a commitment on the part of an organizer or leader to work with other people—on a one-on-one basis—to help them grow beyond themselves and participate as a full citizen in the public life of their community. Chambers began focusing on developing strong personal relationships with his key organizers and leaders that extended support, encouragement, honest evaluation, and assistance in developing skills that could be used in the public arena.

This internal relationship building was slow, hard, and invisible to the politician, bureaucrat, or businessman who had to deal with the IAF organizations. But without it, the IAF would have died with Saul Alinsky, and to Chambers, it is "why we do what we do."

"If you want to really make democracy work, if you're crazy enough to believe that the democratic system is one worth proving, and if you know that electoral politics doesn't cut it, and if you know you can communicate that to people who have some central values, then it's worth doing," Chambers says. "Saul had the ideas and concepts, but he didn't believe in the mentoring and the tutoring. He'd just throw me in and say, 'don't bother me.'"

Chambers vowed he wouldn't do that to the organizers and leaders he trained. And his concept of "mentoring and tutoring" had a profound effect on Ernie Cortes. When he first went to the IAF, Cortes had the benefit of hours and hours of conversation with the more experienced Chambers. Chambers worked with him on a personal level, helping him integrate his intellectualism with his need for action in the public arena. Later, Chambers assigned another organizer the task to meet with Cortes several times each week.

"As they probed me, I started thinking about how I ought to be doing this too. I was beginning to see that electoral politics just didn't go deep enough, and I began to do some reading to find out how to reach people on a deeper level myself," Cortes says.

Cortes read psychology—Freud and Jung, of course, but also Kohlberg, Karen Horney, Henry Stack Sullivan, Gustav Napier, Murray Brown, and others. He delved into theories of family therapy. To gain insight into women, he studied Doris Lessing's novels and questioned the women he organized. How did they think about themselves? Why were they so hesitant to take on leadership roles? What did they care most about?[6] And he began to incorporate what he was learning, plus his own instincts, into a process of working individually with people to help them discover their strengths and to learn how to use them in a public setting.

By now, Cortes had signed on with the IAF to become a full-time organizer, and he worked on projects in Chicago, Milwaukee, and Lake County, Indiana. Cortes discovered that the people he worked with were amazed to find a community organizer who thought about them in an individual or personal way, and who would actually listen to their ideas and concerns, advise them, develop their public skills, and help them synthesize their reading, reflection, and action. It amazed Cortes, too, and he realized he was involved in a new, more effective way to organize people to act in their own self-interest.

Then in 1973, Cortes decided to go home. His marriage had ended and he wanted to be with his young daughter, Ami, who was in Texas. Besides, change was in the air in San Antonio. The Good Government League was crumbling under the weight of its own inertia in the face of a challenge from a bunch of builders and developers who simply wanted to make money—big money they felt they could make if only the city fathers had guts enough to get out of the country club and annex land, build new sewer and water lines, widen streets—let the city grow! North Side Anglos were tearing each other to shreds, not like gentlemen behind closed doors, but like rowdies for all the city to see. A wealthy former GGL city council member who had been shut out because in his own words, he was "one of the most irreverent bastards you've ever known,"[7] announced as an independent candidate for mayor—and he won. He brought with him a slate of independents who looked like they might break the GGL's hold on the city once and for all.

To Cortes, it seemed like a good time to come home. Maybe the "sleeping giant" was stirring too.

Part Three

Fire, chaos, shadows,
Events trickling from a thin line of flame
On into cries and combustions never expected:
The people have the element of surprise.

Carl Sandburg
The People, Yes

11

Leave Them Alone.
They're Mexicans.

San Antonio, 1973

Father Edmundo Rodriguez was one of those activist priests who seemed to be everywhere.[1] For him, there was no shortage of good causes—civil rights, bilingual education, police brutality, welfare rights. A Jesuit, he once in the 1960s organized an effort to get San Antonio's charity hospital, the Robert B. Green, to set up a grievance committee for its patients. During this effort, Father Rodriguez first met Ernesto Cortes, who was serving on the hospital's board. Now in 1973, an older and probably wiser Father Rodriguez and Ernesto Cortes were talking about developing a new kind of organization on San Antonio's West Side, one that would be different from the dozens of community groups that had sprung to life almost overnight during the Great Society. In the mid-1960s, federal money was free-flowing for VISTA volunteers, Legal Aid programs, Model Cities citizen's groups, community action agencies, and dozens of other ventures with window-dressing requirements for "citizen participation." But the money bags had giant strings attached, some of which were pulled so haphazardly as to cut off the circulation for any legitimate or independent citizen action. The money also created a new class of local bureaucrats whose first loyalty in many cases was to their own livelihood rather than to their less fortunate clients. Cortes wanted none of that. Public money should support public projects—not groups of activists whose independence and integrity could be compromised with high salaries and low accountability. At the Industrial Areas Foundation, Cortes had come to believe wholeheartedly in Alinsky's Iron Rule—never do for people what they can do for themselves.

Father Rodriguez liked the Iron Rule, as well as the other ideas spewing from Cortes' active, volcanic mind. The talks continued over the weeks. Cortes laid out his proposal. Based on what he had learned as an IAF organizer, Cortes envisioned a new San Antonio organization to be built around poor Mexican parishes, like Father Rodriguez's Our Lady of Guadalupe Church on the near West Side, not far from the old Missouri-Pacific Railroad station. This organization would take no federal or local government money, nor would it hustle private foundation grants. Instead, its seed money would come from an ecumenical sponsoring committee, which would closely monitor the project and hold the staff accountable for how money was spent.

All of this could happen if Rodriguez agreed to help, which Rodriguez badly wanted to do. But he had seen political activists come and go in the 1960s. Some even genuinely tried to help poor people get a measure of control over their lives. Cortes himself had come and gone, but now, here he was again. Yet somehow, he was different from the rest of them.

Rodriguez decided to take a chance. Cortes' concept of a wholly self-owned, self-operated organization was a novel one for San Antonio. It might work. And as for Cortes, he seemed eager to apply what he had learned at the IAF to the West Side people whose history and experiences he had imbibed. Rodriguez sensed that Cortes was as ready as he to move beyond the political rhetoric of the 1960s and reach people at a deeper level. Cortes, after all, was talking about appealing to the strong family values of West Side Hispanics and of drawing on the religious language and stories of people whose emotional roots were entwined with the Catholic church. He seemed to recognize that support of the church was essential, particularly because more than 400,000 of San Antonio's 550,000 Catholics were Hispanic.[2] Rodriguez liked that, too. Cortes was the first political operative he had seen who seemed to want the church to participate, as well as provide money.

So Father Rodriguez agreed to help put together a sponsoring committee to raise the money, and Cortes committed himself to a three-year, hands-on organizing effort to give the organization a chance to sink roots deep enough to withstand the stormy winds certain to follow. Rodriguez persuaded then–Auxiliary Catholic Bishop Patrick Flores to serve as a member of the sponsoring committee. But the Protestant members of the committee brought the first real money to the effort. Long familiar with Saul Alinsky's IAF organizing, the Reverend John Moyer of the United Church of Christ and the Reverend Leo Nieto of the United Methodist church were instrumental in raising the first $40,000 for the effort. Father Rodriguez's religious order, the Society of Jesus, gave $3,000. The local Catholic Archdiocese kicked in another $4,000, and later that year, the Catholic church's Campaign for Human Development donated $15,000 to the effort. With this kind of money, the advice of Ed Chambers, which came with a $10,000 contract with the IAF, and the low-overhead operation Cortes proposed, the new organization might have a chance to develop some staying power. Cortes was to be paid $14,000 a year, with only Rodriguez signing checks. The new organization was called the Committee for Mexican American Action. Thus, Cortes settled back into San Antonio, unnoticed by the press, old friends, and most of his political cronies from the 1960s.

Cortes' initial approach was simply to listen. He interviewed pastors of West Side Catholic parishes and got the names of their key layleaders. Cortes was looking for a core group of people around which he could build an organization in each parish. After the parishes were organized, he envisioned an organization of organizations to which the churches would belong, paying dues from their Sunday collections to make the whole effort self-supporting. No outside funding would be necessary. But people constituted organizations, so Cortes' first job was to find the people. He wasn't interested in the activists involved in party politics or the growing band of Chicano radicals whose talk was as shrill as some of the most extreme black power rhetoric. He was not looking for the loose, unconnected

cause-chaser who got a rush from pulling off a successful dem
onstration and who then moved on to the next town or the new
sexy issue. Instead, Cortes was looking for people with ties.
Obligations. He wanted people wrapped up in their parishes,
their jobs, and their children. He wanted men and women who
cared about their neighborhoods and who would have demonstrated that care in hundreds of small, almost anonymous activities. He was looking for "natural" leaders—those who organized their PTAs and church festivals, those who put together
the baseball tournaments and the Boy Scout troops, or those
who served as union stewards and social club presidents. In
each parish, pastors identified for Cortes at least two or three
dozen people who had demonstrated these small but significant
leadership qualities. Cortes began to call on them, one by one,
and nearly everyone he talked to gave him names of even more
prospects.

"We tried to bust the stereotypes . . . to see leaders not necessarily as someone who could speak or persuade a crowd. We
wanted to see leaders as people who have networks, relationships with other people," Cortes says of those days.

To find his core group of leaders, Cortes interviewed more
than a thousand people. Some, like PTA leader and housewife
Beatrice Gallegos, whose daughter had won a Miss Teenage
San Antonio contest, he had to call 17 times before they would
talk to him. Some took to him immediately, like Andres Sarabia,
who was a computer programmer at Kelly Air Force base and
who offered to help in any way. Cortes relied on people like
Sarabia, the parish president of Holy Family Church, to assist
and even inspire him.

"Andy had a real hunger for learning and also a lot of anger.
He was a migrant worker as a child. He lived in the projects and
was very streetwise. He knew how to fight his way out of a bad
situation," Cortes says.

Cortes kept records and tapes of each conversation with Sarabia and all of the others he interviewed. He listened, and he
learned. "I would talk to people for about 30 minutes to an
hour, never longer. I didn't want to impose on their time. I
would run back to my car and put as much of the conversation
as I could remember on note cards. Then I'd head for the next

appointment," Cortes says. "Late at night, I'd read over what people had told me."

Cortes' notes revealed that the altar society presidents and Kelly Field workers did not talk about police brutality. They were not obsessed with civil rights issues. Of course, they knew Mexicans were still discriminated against, and, of course, it bothered them. But what really concerned them more was sending their kids to a school where trash barrels were stationed around the cafeteria to catch rainwater from the leaky roof. They were worried about being unable to pay their electric bills because of the city's skyrocketing utility rates. They were bothered by the glue-sniffing kids hanging out behind the ice-house on the corner. They were upset about the water surging into their yards and homes when it rained. They were frightened by the rats invading their homes from the junkyards down the block. They were tired of the daily inconveniences of inadequate bus service or broken street lights. They were frustrated because there were no parks or neighborhood swimming pools for their kids. And they were angry because no one ever listened to them.

To Father Rodriguez, who had worked for years to get his parishioners involved in politics, Ernie Cortes' organizing reports were "like one of those light bulbs that suddenly appears in cartoons."[3] Father Rodriguez, like many well-meaning activists, had never asked people what they wanted. He just assumed he knew. Ernie Cortes, however, was actually listening to the concerns of families with real bills to pay and real needs to be met each day. He was treating them as individuals whose problems were more important to him than some vague ideological concept of organizing the "masses." Once people figured out that Cortes was not just another poverty program huckster and that he was genuinely interested in how they felt, they responded warmly. When Cortes and their pastors invited them to meetings to talk about how their neighborhood could be improved, they came. In dozens of churches all over the West Side, men and women began to meet and talk, and more importantly, to think.

At the parish meetings, people began to look at how decisions were made in the city. Who determined how much they paid for electricity? Who made the decisions about storm drains? How could they get school administrators to fix leaky roofs? Who were the people outside of government who wielded influence over the public decision-makers? Who got the money resulting from public decisions?

As they got answers to these questions, the West Side church people also discussed their fears about confronting the decision-makers. And once again, Ernie Cortes and Father Edmundo Rodriguez listened and learned. People were not so much afraid of losing their jobs or worried about what their neighbors would think. Those were externals. The fears Cortes discovered were internal, in some ways more basic. People simply didn't want to be made fools of in public by experts who knew more than they did. They could not bear to be humiliated. Because they dreaded dealing with city or school officials, Cortes taught them how to equalize the situation by becoming experts themselves. Parish members learned the value of research. They pored through government documents, city hall reports, minutes of public meetings. They learned to read budgets and financial records and bond covenants. And the more they learned, the angrier they became.

Particularly about drainage. Many times when there was a heavy or prolonged rain in San Antonio, someone died in the swirling flood waters that overflowed the web of drainage ditches and creek beds that criss-crossed the West Side.

San Antonio's West Side was made up of curbless streets with few storm drains. Huge ditches, as wide as city streets, carried off the muddy rainwater rushing down each street. But the ditches were often choked by high grass, rotten lumber, beer cans, old mattresses, abandoned tires—the typical mess of urban refuse. So the flood waters overflowed the ditches, surging through streets and yards and into homes. Year after year, more than 100,000 West Side families were affected by the flooding, many losing their property to the muddy mess and more than a few losing their lives. But beyond the blaring one-day headlines and few mutterings that "something ought to be done," each flood was forgotten until the next one came along. Rain and death. What could you do?

Little by little, the parishioners were learning what to do. Their research began to prove as functional as the blaze on a miner's hat in a dark tunnel. From poring over old documents, they learned that the city of San Antonio had approved bonds for West Side drainage improvements in 1945—and not a penny of that money had ever been spent on the West Side! Now the housewives, church volunteers, youth club leaders, and baseball coaches were outraged. Rain and death need not have been synonymous for the past 30 years!

When the delegates from 27 churches met in the summer of 1974 for their first joint meeting, they made some important decisions. They would put aside the concerns of each individual parish and concentrate on solving one problem plaguing the entire West Side: drainage. Everything else could wait. It was a momentous day for San Antonio, because in addition to deciding to work together for a common goal, these church people also decided to give themselves a new name, one more appropriate for what they wanted to do. The Committee for Mexican American Action just didn't work for them, they agreed. But what would be better? Someone jokingly suggested the name COPS—"You know, they're the robbers and we're the cops." Someone else, mindful of the high utility bills charged by the city's Public Service Board, pointed out that the "PS" in COPS could stand for real public service—"only we would really mean it!"[4] So Communities Organized for Public Service was shaped to fit an acronym, and the COPS were about to hit the streets, ready for action.

But it would not be Ernesto Cortes who would lead them. That was not the plan. Cortes' role all along had been to *train* leaders, not to *be* the leader. As COPS members prepared to go public, Cortes receded into the background. Parish leaders, with Cortes' coaching, set up a meeting with the city manager to talk about the city's drainage problems. They organized their facts, planned the meeting, and rehearsed their presentation.

City manager Sam Granata agreed to meet with COPS members at a West Side high school August 13, 1974. Just five days before the meeting, San Antonio experienced a torrential downpour that drove 40 families from their homes, swept away a bridge over the Mayberry drainage ditch, and made streets all over the West Side impassable. It was a made-to-order disaster, the perfect backdrop for the meeting with city officials. The rain even "bolstered our faith in God," said Andy Sarabia.[5] Five hundred angry COPS members could hardly wait to confront Granata and the city that had condemned them to years of neglect, which they could now prove with facts and figures. At the meeting in the hot and humid school auditorium, COPS leaders told the city manager they were not interested in any of his long-winded explanations. They wanted "simple yes or no answers" to their questions. Why was the West Side so neglected? What had happened to the bond money? Would the city rectify its past mistakes?

One COPS leader showed slides of the recent water damage in a West Side neighborhood and told the manager "scenes like this have been there for years and are still the same. We have decided not to take it anymore. We have decided to make our problem your problem."[6] Granata's explanations were pointless, and he finally admitted to the shouting audience that the city had just flat "dropped the ball." All COPS members had to do, he advised, was simply to "ask" the mayor and city council to pick it up. So COPS asked to be on the city council's agenda the very next week.

Paul Burka, whose *Texas Monthly* article on COPS brought the group widespread attention for the first time in 1977, believes that Granata's ill-advised admission that San Antonio's city government operated by the squeaky-wheel-gets-the-grease method did as much to politicize COPS membership as all of their careful research. "It exploded the myth most of them had accepted for years—that the city in its wisdom would take care of them in good time. The battle lines were drawn for keeps."[7]

The next week at the city council meeting, hundreds of eager COPS members filled the chamber. One council member said afterward that it reminded him of Col. William B. Travis' famous message from the Alamo: "I am besieged with a thousand or more of the Mexicans."[8]

When COPS spokeswoman Mrs. Hector Aleman rose to speak, the entire COPS delegation stood up in the council chambers, and some even crowded close to Mrs. Aleman at the podium to offer her a phalanx of psychological support.

"We are here to demand action," Mrs. Aleman said, speaking slowly in a trembling voice. "We don't want excuses."

As Mrs. Aleman told the story of repeated flooding in her neighborhood, a cluster of homes near Holy Family Catholic

Church, her voice grew louder and stronger. The project to fix her neighborhood's drainage problem had been on the city's master plan since 1945, she explained. But nothing had ever been done. Her neighbors had to fight the floods year after year. Finally she was shouting to the council, "How would you feel getting out of bed in the morning and stepping into a river right in your house?"[9]

Mayor Charles Becker, the self-described "irreverent bastard" who had ousted the Good Government League, was astounded to learn that bonds had been approved 30 years earlier to deal with West Side drainage problems. "Sam, how long has this project been on the books?" he asked City Manager Sam Granata.

"Since 1945, Mayor," Granata responded.

"You mean to tell me this project has been on the city's list that long and never received a thin dime?"

"That's right, Mayor."

"Well, that's a damn shame," the mayor said. Then he asked one more question. "Sam, how many people does this affect?"

"About 40,000, Mayor."

"Well, by God, let's do it."[10]

The mayor gave Granata and the city's staff four hours to come up with a plan to finance the operation. The result was a new $46 million bond issue that voters approved the following November—providing COPS members their first taste of electoral victory. And with it, hundreds of church-going West Side families realized just how hungry they had been.

To Andy Sarabia, who was elected COPS' first president that same month by 2,000 delegates from South and West Side churches, the whole episode was a lesson in political power he never had dreamed possible. "We got into COPS because we cared about our neighborhoods," he said. "We weren't looking for any handouts—we're taxpayers and we found out our tax money wasn't working for us. They'd promise us projects and then they'd use the money for something on the North Side. We found case after case of it. It made us angry. Then we found that they were incompetent. When you learn something emotionally, I guarantee you, you never forget it."[11]

COPS had learned all right, and now it was ready to act. Fresh from its bond election victory for drainage improvements,

COPS proposed a $100 million "counter budget" for the city, detailing project after project for the long-neglected West Side—more drainage improvements, new parks, libraries, chug-hole repair, sidewalks, and street curbs. Mayor Becker, the developers, and the business community were incredulous. Who did these people think they were? It was one thing to complain about flooding and a bureaucratic blunder in the old days, but quite another to have the audacity to propose an entirely new capital expenditure budget for the city of San Antonio!

Becker and the new boys in power in San Antonio simply refused to discuss it, and the media dismissed it as a publicity ploy. Then COPS pulled a series of "actions" that at long last began to arouse the Mexican "sleeping giant" and to establish the organization as a major power player in San Antonio. To let the mayor know it meant business, COPS targeted two of San Antonio's most venerable institutions: Joskes department store and the Frost National Bank. On February 4 and 5, 1975, hundreds of COPS members first went to Joskes, trying on everything in sight and buying nothing. Then, they lined up at the teller windows at the Frost Bank, changing hundreds of dollars into pennies and then back again into dollars. It was chaotic and disruptive, but perfectly legal. Its participants were the men and women who had quietly supported their church and community activities before without so much of a hint that they could be so disruptive of downtown San Antonio commerce.

George Ozuna was 17 when he and his grandmother went downtown the day of the Joskes try-on. "When we got downtown, I saw some kind of demonstration," Ozuna remembers. "So I told my grandmother that we'd have to walk around. She said, 'Oh, no.' It turned out she was part of the whole thing."[12]

While COPS members like the Ozunas were tying up sales clerks and bank tellers, other COPS leaders were holding private meetings to persuade the city's retail and banking executives that it would be in the city's best interest if they persuaded the mayor to meet with COPS on the counter budget. Joskes' manager refused to get involved, and the president of the Frost Bank, Tom Frost, Jr., although very polite to the COPS leaders while their members were occupying his bank lobby, also refused to call the mayor on behalf of COPS. Cortes, who had planned to take a back seat in the negotiations with Frost, couldn't restrain himself as the meeting fell apart.

"My leaders freeze, and they don't do anything," Cortes said. "I believe in the Iron Rule of organizing: never do anything for anybody they ain't doing for themselves. *But they ain't doing for themselves!* They're collapsing; they're folding. Our people are downstairs waiting with no instruction, no word and they don't know what to do. I decide I've got to do something, so I move my chair over to Mr. Frost, and he's got a blood vessel that's exposed, and I focus on it and I look at it. I just keep moving, he moves away, and I move closer with the chair. Then finally he says something, and I say, 'Mr. Frost, that's a bunch of balderdash. You're the most arrogant man I've ever met.' . . . We have a priest there and Mr. Frost says, 'Father, you better teach your people some manners and some values.' And finally the priest says, 'Well, Mr. Frost, I don't know about that, but you know, you're apathetic and I think that's much worse.'"[13]

Meanwhile, television stations carried prime-time news coverage of COPS members trying on furs, shoes, and expensive jewelry and creating lines in the Frost Bank lobby, frightening away hundreds of paying customers who avoided the downtown area altogether. Retailers began to panic. Who knows what these people might do next? Something had to be done. After several days of tense negotiations, the head of the Chamber of Commerce came to see Cortes, hat in hand. But Cortes refused to meet with him alone and delayed any discussion until COPS leaders like Andy Sarabia could be rounded up. After this meeting and others, COPS eventually got the city's commitments for more than $100 million in improvements.

It was gutsy stuff for priests and nuns, housewives, federal civil service employees, and the dozen or so grandmothers who stood their ground with the city fathers. One woman's feelings were typical of the basically conservative West Side residents who were affected by what they were seeing: "I couldn't believe the church was involved. They're always saying 'mind your manners.' How could they support such things? It was just horrible. And I can't figure out to this day what made me change my mind and join COPS."[14]

But George Ozuna's grandmother knew why, even though she got some criticism from old friends for her involvement with COPS. Ozuna says his grandmother told him, "I'm doing this because we're winning. Your grandfather and I came from Mexico to try to build something. But we were losers. There were things that always worked to keep us down. In Mexico, it was the government taking away our animals and chickens. Here it was poverty again. Grandfather working at Finesilver with no union. All my life I've worked very hard to win, to find something where you're really winning. We've always lost. Now I'm winning. *We're* winning. And we have a say-so in what's going on. And we're going to have more of a say-so."[15]

Over the next few years, COPS members showed up at every meeting of the city's planning commission, its water and electric system boards, and, of course, at the weekly city council meetings. And COPS members were not just quiet and meek observers taking notes in the back of the room. They were participants: loud, irreverent, and knowledgeable, cheering their speakers, booing their opponents, taking charge, and refusing to be cowed.

The late Father Albert Benavides,[16] one of the beloved and legendary leaders of the organization, had a great sense of humor and delighted in injecting a little ridicule into the COPS battles with officials. Once, he so infuriated a city council member that he was challenged to "take off that collar and fight like a man." The priest even once took charge of a city council meeting after Lila Cockrell[17] had succeeded Charlie Becker as mayor and had gently tried to spread her lace doily style of leadership over COPS' appearances before the city council. But the doily simply wasn't big enough for the podium:

> Mayor Cockrell: "You asked me a particular question and I know that there are perhaps other council members who would like to speak, and also there may be other citizens and so I don't want to monopolize you."
>
> Father Benavides: "That's all right. This is our time, isn't it?"
>
> Mayor Cockrell: "Yes it is."
>
> Father Benavides: "So, you may continue with your remarks, Mrs. Cockrell."
>
> Councilman Bob Billa: "Father, let me say . . ."
>
> Father Benavides: "Sir, you are out of order; Mayor Cockrell has the floor."[18]

Another COPS leader, Ramon Castillo, was thrown out of a council meeting by the flustered Mayor Cockrell because he refused to stop his belligerent questioning of council members about a secret meeting over the city's lawsuit against its gas supplier. And 1,000 COPS members delayed a public hearing for 20 minutes on the settlement of that same lawsuit with their jeers, shouts, and stomping. Mayor Cockrell and people who served as chairs of other city boards and commissions sometimes got so frustrated they recessed their meetings in mid-shout. But that didn't always work either. One time, Andy Sarabia and a group of COPS women followed a state water official to lunch because he had refused to answer their questions in the public meeting. They stood over his table as he ate, demanding answers to their questions. Sarabia later joked that the incident wasn't quite as daring as it appeared. "Do you think anybody would arrest 100 middle-aged Mexican-American women and a big-mouth male?" he said.[19]

Polite, refined San Antonio officials didn't know what to do. These people weren't playing by their rules: waiting their turn, showing respect. Reaction to COPS' bellicose tactics was as strong as the reaction to COPS' demands. Chamber of Commerce officials claimed that San Antonio was being discredited throughout the nation because COPS disrupted public meetings with "taunts, threats, disrespect and harassment."[20] But whereas COPS threats were political, some of their leaders were receiving threats that became dangerously personal. "When I received a phone call telling me not to start the car in the morning, I knew we had found the jugular vein," Andy Sarabia said.[21]

But COPS would not stop, shut up, or drop its confrontational tactics. Why quit the only thing that had worked in 30 years? The confrontations forced city officeholders and power brokers to deal with COPS' issues, and they created an atmosphere that made it impossible to continue discrimination and neglect. "If we had kept on whispering, no one would have ever heard," Sarabia said.[22]

The San Antonio *News* agreed in a 1976 editorial: "While COPS disruptive tactics have become predictable, tiresome and increasingly unnecessary, the group has . . . exposed city fathers to feelings and viewpoints . . . heretofore ignored by City Hall.

That's good. Participatory democracy, while often upsetting, is what this country is about."[23]

For the first time in San Antonio, the television cameras were showing ordinary people standing up to the politicians to present their grievances, and the cameras showed that it was not the poor people who looked uncomfortable and uneasy; instead, it was the politicians.

The tactics may not have played well in the business district or on the Anglo North Side, but they were a big hit on the predominately black East Side, as well as on the city's South Side, which was composed of working-class whites and an expanding population of Hispanics. And the West Side was positively euphoric. Especially when someone like Inez Ramirez, a petite mother of 10 children, took on the city manager. "Heavens knows what you would do if you were in our shoes," she told the city's top appointed official. "But you wouldn't fit . . . our shoes are much too small. They make our toes hurt, and give us headaches and make us sick to our stomachs. We're taxpayers, too, yet people wake up in the morning in our districts with snakes in the bedroom from poor housing and rats in the bathroom from the junkyards. We have no parks or recreation centers so our children are forced to find 'amusement' in secluded areas where they must associate with the glue sniffers and dope peddlers. We want our fair share of city revenue for our projects. And if we don't get them, you and maybe all of us are going to hell."[24]

Cab drivers, beauticians, waitresses, teachers, ice-house clerks, truck drivers, and grandmothers and grandfathers felt proud when they heard COPS leaders like Mrs. Ramirez. They laughed at the antics of Father Benavides and cheered at the confrontations, telling each other "it's about time." The only way to be a member of COPS was to be a member of your church, and West Side Catholic parishes came alive with activity. Members wore their COPS buttons proudly, as a badge of honor. Sister Christine Stephens tells how she learned the power of those COPS buttons once when she was in San Antonio for a meeting of her religious order, the Community of Divine Providence (CDP). When she stopped on the West Side to get gasoline for her car, the attendant mistook the CDP button of her sisterhood for a COPS button. "Ah, I see you're a member of COPS," he said with admiration. "I love COPS."

Each day's newscast carried COPS into every San Antonio household. The organization had a higher name identification than any politician in the city. One radio station even ran a regular COPS calendar to let listeners know where the next COPS action would be taking place.

Serious changes were occurring in San Antonio, and COPS was helping interpret them in front of the news cameras for the entire city. With the end of the Good Government League and business monopoly and the failure of the developers who took the GGL's place to build any credible political organization, the city was wide open. Anything was possible. For the first time in 25 years, there was an immense power vacuum, which COPS proceeded to fill. And if it was chaotic and troublesome for some, it was also exhilarating for others. Before one COPS meeting, San Antonio *Express-News* columnist Roddy Stinson advised readers to hold everything: "If you're thinking of committing suicide, wait—this could be fun!"[25]

In 1976, COPS joined with the environmentally concerned North Siders who had formed the Aquifer Protection Association to gather 48,000 signatures on petitions forcing an election over the city council's decision to allow a shopping mall to be built on land covering the city's great underground reservoir, the Edwards Aquifer, which stretched more than 175 miles across South Central Texas. COPS, with its massive West Side voter registration and get-out-the-vote drive, was credited with getting voters to reject the mall. The next year, after a federal court decision struck down the at-large system of electing city council members, COPS forces won a city charter election that created 10 single-member districts, with the mayor elected at large. In the following election, five Hispanic candidates won council seats. With the vote of a black council member elected from the city's East Side, minorities in San Antonio constituted a majority in city government for the first time. Young city council member Henry Cisneros, who had first been elected to the council in 1975 with GGL support, saw the shift in power and began to cultivate COPS leaders.

Neither this new council majority, however, nor the

subsequent councils over the years guaranteed COPS smooth sailing for all of its proposals. But the more democratic structure of city government did allow an organization like COPS to operate on an equal level with wealthy developers or with the downtown Chamber of Commerce or with the affluent North Side professionals whose political sophistication seemed to come with their territory. Little by little, the local parish groups that comprised COPS came to be considered the dominant element in the always seesawing political atmosphere in San Antonio. Because of a more receptive city government and a generally more friendly press, which could easily document the major municipal improvements generated by COPS, the organization no longer had to resort to its more raucous tactics—or at least, not so often.

COPS became as adroit as the old GGL in directing money and media attention to what it perceived to be the needs of the city. With money from local voter-approved bonds, as well as Community Block Development Grants and other federal sources, COPS got the city to channel more than $500 million in capital improvements to West and South Side neighborhoods. There were new libraries, swimming pools, sidewalks, bridges, street lights, and curbs. Dilapidated structures were removed, and debris was hauled away from vacant lots. Storm drains were put in place, and people didn't die when it rained. New housing sprang up, and old neighborhoods were refurbished. West Side schools improved their student-to-teacher ratio, and bilingual education programs became standard.

The city's wide-open growth policies, which were adopted during the four-year period when the developers controlled city hall, were moderated, and massive city subsidies for developers, such as free materials for water mains, were eliminated. Although growth management remained a hot topic for the city, developers found out it was cheaper and less time consuming if they dealt with COPS' concerns up front—rather than by attempting city hall end runs around the organization and its increasingly sophisticated leaders.

Because of a furor raised by COPS, San Antonio no longer advertised itself as a "cheap labor" town. In fact, COPS turned the city's economic development activities upside down, and city boosters began seeking new business and industry that provided good-paying jobs for its citizens.

In short, there was a change in the way the city and its players conducted business. Astute political observers gave COPS the lion's share of the credit. Even when it occasionally lost a battle, as it did now and then, COPS did not fade away, fall apart, or feed on itself. A new president was elected every two years, and new leaders took their place at the city hall podium to challenge the mayors and council members. COPS itself still accepted no public money and kept close to its church base. And except for one brief flirtation with endorsing candidates in 1977, after a West Side city council candidate made his opposition to COPS the central feature of his campaign, COPS maintained no formal ties with officeholders, candidates, or political parties and never endorsed candidates in any race. Yet COPS continued to shape public events in San Antonio. Even after Ernie Cortes left San Antonio in 1976 to start a similar organization in East Los Angeles, COPS continued. It was not dependent on him or any other single individual.

By 1976, the San Antonio *Light* had placed COPS on its list of the 10 most powerful in San Antonio, and the city council itself recognized COPS' power on the organization's 10th anniversary in 1983 by proclaiming "COPS week" and saying that "COPS has been a model and a testimony to our democratic values and the richness of cultural heritage in our city."[26] The San Antonio *Light* editorialized, "If COPS is at times too vocal, other organizations need but take note that vocal protest in orderly fashion is the backbone of democracy."[27] And Henry Cisneros, whose election in 1981 as the first Hispanic mayor of San Antonio in 150 years can be directly attributed to his relationship with COPS and the new political climate it established in the city, told COPS members on their 10th anniversary, "Thank you for what you have done for my city."[28] Even banker Tom Frost, the target of COPS' infamous bank penny exchange, admitted that COPS had turned out to be "good for the city." Developer Jim Dement agreed: "There's more hope and conversation in this town than in a hundred years. . . . This is a town where you can have nothing and be somebody. Now don't tell me COPS is bad."[29]

Current Catholic Archbishop Patrick Flores, who served on the original sponsoring committee that provided money and support to get COPS started and gave Pope John Paul II a COPS button, called COPS the "soul of San Antonio."[30] The archbishop was referring as much to the intangible changes in San Antonio as to the cement and pipe public improvements credited to the COPS balance sheet.

Middle-class Mexican-Americans began staying on the West Side even when they could afford to move north. For some, the lure of an involved public life became stronger than the lure of a North Side neighborhood. "There is a conscious choice made by nearly everybody who associates themselves with COPS not to bail out of the West Side," said Sister Maribeth Larkin, who served as COPS' lead organizer for two years.[31]

George Ozuna is one of the younger generation of Mexican-Americans who have decided to stay on the West Side even though he could afford to live anywhere in town. After attending graduate school at the University of Texas, he says he decided to return to the West Side because of something his grandmother told him. "You can go to college to get away from your community or you can learn something to come back and make a contribution," she said.[32] Ozuna came back and represents the third generation of his family to be touched by COPS. In addition to his grandmother, his mother Patricia Ozuna has been an articulate co-chair of the organization.

"People now have hope," Ozuna said. "There is a sense that things will get better. COPS gives me a sense of power—that we can do something, that we can change our lives, that we have an impact on our future. That used to be in the hands of someone else. Now it is in our hands. Now we control our destiny."[33]

The possibility of controlling their destiny was an especially powerful lure for the Hispanic women who became leaders in COPS. From the beginning, the women did most of the research. They set up the meetings, made the telephone calls, and got out the vote. They recruited their neighbors and organized the projects. Because the IAF philosophy correlated leadership with "producing results," women were rewarded for their efforts over the years by being elected to positions of leadership within COPS—including the powerful and visible top job as COPS' president. Holding office gave them the opportunity to make presentations before the city council, challenge officials at accountability sessions, or be interviewed on television. It was a new role for Hispanic women, who, with few exceptions, had never become active politically or in the women's movement. Now, women like Beatrice Cortez, Carmen Badillo, Beatrice Gallegos, Sonia Hernandez, and others who served as presidents of COPS were recognized political leaders.

Their husbands, fathers, and sons cheered them along. One leader said that as long as people looked at COPS as a neighborhood organization, it was fine for women to be the leaders. "In the Mexican culture, women have the responsibility for home and children," she said. "Schools related to children. Neighborhood is a part of home. So, if a woman raises hell about drainage in the neighborhood, that's okay."[34]

Ernie Cortes believes that women were attracted to COPS because it offered them the chance to develop the "public" side of their lives. "Many of the women leaders were real powerhouses in their private families," he says. "They had a lot to say about who does what. But that's not enough. The public side of them didn't get developed because they are invisible outside of the home. They may have gravitated to leadership in our organization because of the need to develop this aspect of their personality. We offered them the opportunity."

COPS also made a difference in the behavior of politicians. Even though COPS decided not to endorse candidates, COPS members knew who their friends were, and San Antonio politicians learned to count votes. A major COPS get-out-the-vote effort could generate from 40,000 to 50,000 votes, and some COPS precincts showed 90 percent of eligible voters to be registered. And the membership dues and fundraising drives that make up COPS' estimated $150,000 annual budget have given the organization the financial stability to maintain its clout.

E.D. Yoes, Jr., writing in the *Texas Observer,* believes that COPS' effect on politicians goes even deeper than the threat of its votes. "Just by being on hand for every meeting and keeping score on who votes how, COPS has had a remarkable clarifying effect on what was once one of the muddier political puddles in Texas, characterized by backroom deals, inexplicable shifting alliances, ill-defined positions on issues and soothing syrup ladled out during campaigns," he wrote.[35]

But an organization like COPS cannot survive unless it does more than tally votes and bird-dog recalcitrant officeholders. Without something deeper, the members of this oldest and most successful community action organization in the nation would have become nothing more than action junkies, watching themselves on the evening news and dreaming up one outrageous stunt after another. Short-lived imitators like ROBBED and the MISSIONS in San Antonio, which came up with little more than single issues and imaginative acronyms, and similar groups in dozens of other American cities have found this out the hard way. Demonstrations, meetings, and confrontations get old. You don't turn hundreds—even thousands—of people out for public hearings and rallies or other events year after year unless they get something personal or even profound out of it. But they kept coming back in San Antonio because COPS put into practice a new kind of politics that transcended neighborhoods to unite people with people, and individuals with their own deepest aspirations. COPS has not gotten old at all.

Beatrice Gallegos, a president of COPS from 1976 to 1978, wrote of what it meant to the individuals who participated. "Not only has the organization changed the city of San Antonio, it has changed us as individuals. It has developed us to make us better persons in our own families, in our churches and in our communities."[36]

Many COPS members also felt that they were fulfilling a larger spiritual purpose and meaning by staying involved. To Andy Sarabia, the "glue that keeps COPS together is no great mystery. It's a faith in our God and in ourselves."[37]

Inez Ramirez, the mother of 10 children who spent most of her life washing clothes and fixing meals before getting involved in COPS and learning how to stand up to public officials, clearly believed it provided her with a mission: "This is not merely politics we are engaged in, but correcting injustice, which is God's work and the mission of the church. There is more to our spirituality than just going to Mass on Sundays. Our spirituality embodies a deep concern for the physical well-being of every individual."[38]

And to Father Edmundo Rodriguez who helped start it all,

"The big change is in the perception expressed by more and more people—it shocks me, in a sense—people keep saying, 'We are the church.' They are savoring something. San Antonio has strong parish councils, which now share power with pastors, where people are really trying to understand the responsibility of the church community."[39]

The occasion of COPS' 10th convention in 1983 was used to evaluate its past and plan its future. Ernie Cortes returned to San Antonio for the celebration, and for the first time, he spoke at length publicly about the meaning of the organization in his address to 10,000 cheering members.

> Today San Antonio is one of the most open cities in America. It is a place where the values of pluralism, family and freedom of speech and assembly have become a concrete reality. . . . But your work is not done. You will be great if and only if you are faithful to the vision upon which you were founded—to teach those who have no stake, no role, and no status how to participate responsibly and effectively in the promise of American life, to have self-respect, dignity, and self-worth. . . . You reach out to those who are outcast. . . . You bring people who are outside democratic society into the life of the community, and you become an instrument whereby they can develop dignity and self-respect. . . . You have truly shown us the real meaning of the Burning Bush, of the fire that never goes out, of the passion for justice that can never be squelched.[40]

Besides Cortes' public appearance, COPS' 10th convention became a political milestone for other reasons. The existence of the hookup between COPS and organizations patterned after them in other Texas cities was acknowledged for the first time with the unveiling of the Interfaith Network, signifying a unified, coordinated approach to issues that could be dealt with only on a statewide level. And the presence of representatives from Brooklyn, Queens, and Los Angeles, who were also building organizations patterned after COPS, revealed more fundamentally than ever before the role of the Industrial Areas Foundation in the support and sustenance of these citizens' organizations.

But it all comes back to San Antonio and the "black hand," the old families, the poverty, and the fear. At COPS' 10th convention, Andy Sarabia summed it up this way:

> Ten years ago, the city leaders said, "Leave them alone. They're Mexicans. They can't organize." Today we have power, we have our culture, we have our faith, we have our communities, we have our dignity, and we're still Mexicans. They feared the successful revolution we started that changed San Antonio from a government of the few by the few to a government of the people by the people and for the people. The significance is that the powerless do not have to stay powerless.[41]

12

A Theology That Does Not Stop

Los Angeles, 1976

Sister Maribeth Larkin has only a small role to play today at city hall when members of a new East Los Angeles community group make their presentation to the city council. All she has to do is to translate from Spanish to English the words of the local leaders who will present the concerns of the United Neighborhoods Organization (UNO) to the council. But she is queasy. Fear grips her stomach, and the telephone call from Ernesto Cortes doesn't help.

"I'm testing you out," Cortes tells her. "We'll see how well you do today and then decide how we can use you." That's all the shy and slender, clear-eyed Sister of Social Service needs to lose her breakfast, even consider calling in sick. How can she possibly stand up and talk in front of the politicians and news media in the chambers of the Los Angeles City Council? Yet, how could she even consider backing out with so many people depending on her? Once again, fear and duty—the hallmarks of her life—provoke conflict within Maribeth Larkin. As usual, duty wins the battle, but the fear remains and turns to panic when she and almost 200 UNO members arrive to see that the council chambers are already full.

It is Larkin's first visit to a Los Angeles City Council meeting, and she is amazed to see hundreds of people filling the pews and leaning against the walls. When it is the turn of UNO representatives and Larkin to make their presentation, they move uncertainly to the podium, waiting for the council members to finish visiting among themselves, sit down, and listen. But the officeholders continue their discussions, oblivious to the dozen or so UNO representatives who stand at the podium. When the first UNO leader begins to speak, Larkin realizes the microphone has been turned off. No one, not even the people within a few feet of the podium, can hear what she is saying. Then, something unusual happens to shy, retiring Sister Maribeth Larkin. She throws away her script, rushes to the front of her group, and begins shouting. "Mr. President . . . Mr. President . . . we've all come here, we deserve a hearing. Could you tell the members of the council who are wandering around to please sit down."

The Catholic sister is yelling at the top of her lungs. She feels sick as a dog, but she is ready to wreak havoc today on any politician who treats her like one. Maribeth Larkin is determined to get the attention of the council president if she has to scream all day. She nails him with her eyes, thinking that if only he would look at her, he would see how serious she is. Which he finally does, and her gaze obviously jolts him, because he turns on the microphone, and council members take their seats. UNO speaks.

Larkin's outburst was as surprising to her as to the members of the Los Angeles City Council. She didn't realize that the wandering around, joke-telling, paper-shuffling, and lack of attention to speakers was the usual demeanor at city hall. It just didn't seem right to her, or fair to UNO members who had been practicing their presentation for weeks. Uncharacteristically for this demure Catholic nun, she reacted angrily to what she saw.

"I didn't know I could do it . . . I didn't know I could speak extemporaneously," she says later. "I got so angry I surprised myself. It was a revelation to me. But I don't think I could have done it had I not had a reservoir of anger bottled up over the years. My outburst at this meeting helped me become free once and for all from my past."[1]

Part of Sister Maribeth Larkin's anger arose from her three-year experience in a poor Los Angeles parish where the pastor had displayed very little concern for his members. Larkin considered six priests in the parish lazy and indifferent. "They even complained about having to take telephone duty one day each week," she says. Larkin's job was to provide free food support for needy parishioners. Because she didn't want them to become dependent on the parish's food program, many of her efforts were spent in finding ways to help them get off food support and become self-sustaining. But her efforts were useless. The pastor of the church would simply hand out $50 here and there to keep from having to deal with the people or listen to their problems. It was an easy way out for the priest, the church, and especially the poor. But it distressed and angered Maribeth Larkin. After only three months in the parish, she requested a transfer. To her dismay, the head of her religious order denied it, telling the sister to "tough it out." It was three years before Larkin was assigned to another church, still feeling hopeless about changing anything. But in her new parish assignment, she worked with a priest who had affiliated his church with UNO, the new Industrial Areas Foundation organization patterned after COPS in San Antonio. He sent Larkin to the IAF's national training program where she had an "awakening" about her own powerlessness within the Los Angeles Archdiocese—as well as within her own middle-class family.

Larkin grew up in Long Beach where her father was an oil company executive and her mother a chemistry teacher. Within her family, conflict was always squelched in order to keep peace—at any price. Larkin became the family peacemaker, smoothing over problems, balancing emotions, and walking a tightrope to keep everyone happy. Both within her own family and her religious order, Larkin systematically smothered her own instincts and resentments, suffering both petty and large injustices unflinchingly. But no more. After the IAF training program, Larkin began to learn about genuine self-interest, power, and the Iron Rule. And the exciting thing to Maribeth Larkin was that what she was learning was being duplicated in dozens of Catholic parishes all over Hispanic East Los Angeles. She began discovering kindred spirits among priests, nuns, and other church leaders. She found people who were willing to question traditional approaches to working with the poor. A new energy was fermenting within the Catholic church, and Larkin felt very much a part of the change that was occurring.

The IAF came to Los Angeles in the mid-1970s when Auxiliary Bishop Juan Arzube, vicar for the Spanish speaking in the archdiocese, had visited San Antonio to take part in programs at the Catholic church's Mexican American Cultural Center. While there, he witnessed some of COPS' activities firsthand, and he had been impressed. COPS booster, San Antonio's Archbishop Patrick Flores, encouraged Arzube to hire an IAF-trained organizer to start a venture in Los Angeles. Convinced that a COPS-like organization would succeed in the barrios of East Los Angeles because of similarities to San Antonio, Bishop Arzube put together a sponsoring committee and raised about $100,000 for the effort.

Like COPS, UNO from its inception entered into an annual contract with the IAF for training and advice. Ed Chambers assisted in the initial fundraising as he had with COPS. When Bishop Arzube asked for help in Los Angeles in 1976, Chambers began persuading Ernie Cortes to give up COPS and move to Los Angeles. It would be a risk for Cortes, and particularly for COPS. If Cortes' personality had been indelibly stamped on COPS, there could be no replacement for him, and the organization he created would fade away. Three years of the most successful IAF organizing since Alinsky's death would go down the drain. But IAF theory and training was designed to prevent just that. Its emphasis on developing new leaders was supposed to keep people and organizations from becoming dependent on any one individual. Now, with Los Angeles calling Cortes, it was time to find out if the theory and training really worked. Could COPS survive without Cortes? And more importantly for Los Angeles, could Cortes duplicate his successes in COPS? The only way to find out would be to try it, which Cortes agreed he must do.

Cortes left San Antonio in 1976, taking with him his COPS-tested ideas. It was to be a fortuitous move. San Antonio had provided Cortes the opportunity to practice his ideas about working closely with people to help them develop public leadership skills, and Los Angeles would provide him the opportunity at last to integrate his theology into the organizing process.

In Los Angeles, the religious pieces began to come together—almost by accident.

The priest of a member parish of UNO complained to Cortes that the organizing efforts were not reaching the entire congregation. UNO was simply not at the center of church concerns. Working men and women, tired and apathetic, saw no compelling spiritual reason to do more than attend Mass. Why should they participate in an effort to end bank redlining of their neighborhoods or to bring down local property insurance rates? What did that have to do with the church? Cortes had to come up with answers, not for his own intellectual satisfaction as he had always been able to do, but for the working poor in the barrios of East Los Angeles.

"Although we organized through the parishes for COPS, I had no real framework or theology of it in a conscious way then," Cortes explains. "In San Antonio we were trying to bring it as close as we could to the life of the parish, and a lot of significant things were happening to people on a spiritual level, but it was all kind of in smithereens. It occurred only when the pastors or the people showed some interest. But I had not worked out a strategy for synthesizing it into the organizing process."

Cortes had all along tried to get people to see themselves as part of a corporate entity—the church—and not as mere individuals. But now, he was being asked to do more. Cortes began reviewing his own experiences as a teacher within COPS, and he tried to identify the training and direct political experiences that had seemed to touch people spiritually. He sorted, sifted, and searched.

"When I was organizing COPS, I would have these late-night discussions with Father Albert Benavides. I had read a book by S.G.F. Brandon—*Jesus and the Zealots*. And I'd throw out Brandon, and Benavides would come back at me saying Brandon didn't really know scripture and I didn't know what that meant. So I kept reading," Cortes explains. "Benavides and Father John Linskins of the Mexican American Cultural Center opened a whole world of scriptural scholarship for me. Toward the end of the COPS experience, I began to pull together some priests for once-a-week sessions to talk about organizing. And we'd talk about the philosophy of it and we'd push each other and talk about the theology of it. One of the priests got up one night and said, 'This is the only time we've ever talked about our own experience of God.' And he was angry with all of the other priests. It created a lot of tension and one of the old guys said, 'Next time, let's talk more organizing and less theologizing.' So we dropped it," Cortes laughingly remembers.

But the priests in Los Angeles were hungry for more "theologizing," so Cortes and the priests came up with an idea for a workshop that put community organizing into a biblical context, using the themes of Pentecost and Sinai as the two central events in the Judeo-Christian tradition. UNO leaders felt that both were especially relevant to people in East Los Angeles because both events drew on the biblical concept of relationship between a *people* and God, in addition to an *individual* and God.

"The concept we were trying to develop was one of community, communal responsibility," he says. Cortes had always believed that Hispanic parishioners felt responsible for their neighbors in a personal way. They took care of each other, responding warmly if someone were sick or out of work. "What we had to do was to get people to go beyond those personal feelings to find out what it was they had in common," he says. "We wanted to get them to extend their personal concerns to the common community. Then, they could build healing relationships and act together on their baptismal vows to be priest, prophet, and shepherd to each other *as a community*."

The challenge was to find a practical way to do this. Cortes had learned from his readings and conversations with Father Albert Benavides that the most powerful way to express that sense of "divine" or the "infinite" that constitutes a religious experience is through symbols and symbolic language—which abound in the Bible and church liturgy.

"Albert brought home to me how important the symbols were to people, how deep they went. But it had to be *their* symbols, *their* stories. As an organizer, I had to be engaged and learning from them at the same time I was trying to teach," Cortes says. And so he began to draw on the old Bible stories in his training sessions, giving them a contemporary twist to reflect what was going on in the lives of East Los Angeles church people.

In the Old Testament, the story of the exodus of the Jews from Egypt and the 40 years of wandering in the desert provided a lesson in the forging of a people despite hardship, despair, and the apparent impossibility of their situation. The acceptance of the commandments delivered to Moses and the establishment of the covenant between God and Israel led to action—the building of a nation. In the New Testament, the story of Pentecost symbolized the decision to begin the church, the decision to act on belief. Forty days after the death of Jesus, the disciples and the faithful gathered to celebrate Pentecost, a Hebrew festival that also commemorated the giving of the Law to Moses on Sinai. As the apostle Peter preached on this day, the despair and confusion over the physical loss of Jesus was miraculously lifted. Belief in the resurrection of Jesus infused the small band with a commitment to act—to build the church.

Cortes discovered in both the stories of Sinai and Pentecost a direct link between belief and action. Action gave value to the belief as well as dignity to the people who carried out the action. Action, then, flowed from idea to deed. But the stories of Sinai and Pentecost also pointed out that action was not just individual heroics. It was "action in community." The action established a relationship with other people—both to work for the common cause and to recruit others to join them in it.

"Both Pentecost and Sinai meant that there was a new political reality," Cortes believes. "The two pivotal events in the Judeo-Christian tradition were the creation of these new communities. And that's what had to be our vision. We had to figure out how to recreate these new communities which are active and changing and transforming the world."

By focusing on the "community" aspects of these age-old biblical stories, Cortes and the UNO priests brought something new to their retelling—at least for the parishioners in East Los Angeles. The UNO sponsoring committee wanted its members to see that not only were they part of the church, they *were* the church. All members of the church suffered when one suffered. And to protect the church, they had to protect each other. As such, the work of the church—*their* work—was here and now in the community. To further reinforce the idea of "action in community," Cortes used Paul's letters to the Corinthians as a teaching tool because he felt they emphasized the decision to mold individual Christians into a community that both nurtured its members and carried its message collectively to the world.

In one Los Angeles parish training session after another, Cortes tried out his new approach. When an idea worked, he expanded on it; when people failed to respond, he probed deeper. Gradually, working with priests, nuns, and layleaders, he developed a training program that provided a solid scriptural basis for the development of community and of the extension of religious belief as a framework for public action.

"Scripturally, there is no separation between body and soul," Cortes believes. "If you separate the body and soul, the important spiritual work of men and women becomes only 'otherworldly.' But if there is a unity, there is also this world. And action must be taken to make this world worthwhile."

Under Cortes' direction, parish members studied not only the idea of community in Paul's letters, but also the idea of leadership in the context of the Beatitudes and in the story of Moses. They would role-play a biblical story—take the situation and see it in the context of their own times, their neighborhood, their relationships, and their community. As they did, they developed an understanding and affinity not only for the particular biblical message, but for its relevance to their own lives and for their capacity as spiritual beings who were capable of taking action. In the role-playing sessions, the small groups would discuss the situation. Then, they would place themselves at the scene but talk and act as themselves. The dialogue that arose during the role-play forged some shared, and often dramatic, experiences among parish members. The understanding they developed for each other in this process helped end their isolation from each other, and they began to develop a vision of community in which they initiated action instead of waiting passively for something—good or bad—to happen to them. "The point was to help people find holiness, to find integrity in their lives," Cortes explains.

East Los Angeles parish members were so excited after these sessions, Cortes recalls, that they kept asking, "Why haven't we done this before?" Cortes felt this was a significant question for people who still looked to the church for guidance in making their lives meaningful, for help with their children or problems with work. "The great thing was that the priests kept encouraging them along," Cortes says.

"I was in parishes where people felt they had never understood the implications of the gospel until they got into this organizing effort," Cortes says. "Then, they understood the dimension of faith in life."[2]

At the same time that UNO leaders were developing the scripturally based parish programs, Cortes was challenged on a different level. His efforts to recruit Sister Maribeth Larkin to become a full-time organizer for the IAF had run into a stumbling block. The leaders of her religious order, the Sisters of Social Service, saw no correlation between the IAF's style of community organizing and their own mission to provide trained social workers to serve the poor. But it was important to Larkin that she be allowed to remain a member of her religious community while taking on IAF organizing duties, and Cortes developed a workshop for her superiors to explain what he felt to be the theological basis for organizing poor people. For these women religious, he had to weave in the doctrinal teachings of the Catholic church, as well as the messages of the Bible.

Cortes went to the papal encyclicals, the letters of the bishops, and other teaching tools of the Catholic church. The encyclicals, in particular, represented a "tradition of sane and humane social thought."[3] Pope Leo XIII's *Rerum Novarum* (*Of New Things*) issued in 1891 was the cornerstone of modern Catholic social thought, giving sanctity to the rights of workers to participate in the organized labor movement. Numerous encyclicals in the almost 100 years since then had expanded the call for a just social and economic order, building on three basic principles of Catholic social thought: 1) a need to protect the dignity of the person, 2) a concern that organizations be no larger than necessary, and 3) the need to have intermediaries between the person and the state—intermediaries like the family, the church, labor unions, voluntary associations—the types of institutions that are always destroyed by totalitarian states.[4]

Even conservative Pope John Paul II's later encyclical on work issued in 1982, *Laborem Exercens*, built on this tradition by placing the root cause of evil in society within its economic institutions and the oppressive conditions they spawned. The Pope's encyclical leaned heavily on the sociology of alienation and proposed an economic system in which people work together for their collective self-interest in "context of the wider consideration of justice for all."[5]

For Cortes, the development of the neighborhood, church-based organization fulfilled the spirit of the church's official documents, and by including the documents in his training sessions for the sisters, he was able to convince them that community organizing could indeed be an outgrowth of the church's concern for the poor and that it could enrich peoples' lives in a religiously significant way.

Cortes began to extend these sessions to both the clergy and laity in parishes throughout East Los Angeles. Their effect spread like wildfire. "The last months I spent with UNO, this was about all I did," Cortes says.

That the sessions were in such demand in Los Angeles reflected not only Cortes' growing theological expertise, but a hunger within the Catholic church for a way to mix theory and action, or praxis. The Catholic church in Latin America and Europe was coming alive with the lay activities of the *communidades de base,* the grass-roots communities of laypeople that shared common liturgical experiences, examined their daily lives and their community in light of biblical messages, and used their analysis as the basis for engagement in the larger community. Some of these lay church communities originated in Europe in the mid-1960s after the impetus of Vatican II, and they revitalized the church in France, Italy, Germany, Poland, Holland, and Spain. But in Latin America, particularly in Brazil where 80,000 such groups existed, they exploded—first as an effort to train layleaders to carry out basic church functions because of a severe shortage of priests, and later as a grass-roots challenge to the political, economic, and even the religious establishment that kept Latin Americans enmeshed in some of the most horrible poverty in the world.

In 1968, the bishops of Latin America assembled in Medellin, Colombia, for a historic conference signifying a turning point in the church. With the blessing of Pope Paul, who was present at the meeting, the bishops issued a letter that became the manifesto of a "new church" committed to the social transformation of Latin America, where nine of 10 people were Catholics and eight of 10 were poor. Two key words emerged at Medellin: liberation and participation.[6]

Liberation was understood in the biblical sense of physical and spiritual salvation—the Exodus in the Old Testament and the Good News proclaimed by Christ in the New Testament. It meant physical freedom from poverty and political repression, and it meant spiritual transformation by taking personal responsibility for spreading the gospel message. The route to liberation and salvation, the bishops said, was through education and participation. Adopting the theories of Brazilian philosopher Paulo Freire, who believed that even the poorest peasant is capable of looking critically at his or her world and acting to improve it, the bishops took the position that to understand salvation, the people first had to become aware of themselves and their environment and to learn to think.[7] Participation in small, parish-based, grass-roots Christian communities provided the opportunity for even the poorest of the poor to develop an understanding of their day-to-day experiences and the causes of their poverty, illiteracy, and subjugation. The Medellin documents turned out to be a revolutionary call for social justice in Latin America and for the first time placed the church in opposition to the military juntas and ruling oligarchies that had institutionalized both social privilege and poverty.

When the work of an intellectual Peruvian priest, Gustavo Gutierrez, was published in 1971 and later translated into English in 1973, church activists committed to the liberation and participation of the poor had a theological framework to pursue direct political action based both in scripture and sociology. In *A Theology of Liberation, History, Politics and Salvation,* Gutierrez had written:

> This is a theology which does not stop with reflecting on the world, but rather tries to be part of the process through which the world is transformed. It is a theology which is open—in the protest against trampled human dignity, in the struggle against the plunder of the vast majority of people, in liberating love, and in the building of a new, just and fraternal society—to the gift of the kingdom of God.[8]

And more directly: "To oppress the poor is to offend God himself; to know God is to work justice among men. We meet God in our encounter with men; what is done for others is done for the Lord."[9]

The cornerstone of Gutierrez's theology, like that of most 20th century theologians, was that salvation for a Christian was not "otherworldly," in which the present life was merely a test. He believed that salvation, which he defined as "the communion of men with God and the communion of men among themselves," embraced and transformed human reality and, when centered in the life of Jesus, allowed people to find fulfillment here and now as complete human beings. Sin for Gutierrez was a breach of man's communion with man. As such, sin was real, here and now, rooted in the history of the exploitation, violence, neglect, and humiliation that people—and governments—used to subjugate the poor and weak. This kind of focus leads to the emphasis—and obligation—to right the historical wrongs and restore communion among people and with God.

The Liberation Theology's emphasis on reflection, analysis, action, and the development of personhood within the supportive confines of small Christian communities obviously influenced Ernie Cortes, as well as the Catholic clergy who clamored for his organizing sessions. But Cortes maintained an arm's length from any public, or private, association with Liberation Theology. "We had some difficulties with it," Cortes says. "It's too analytical, too sociological, coming too much out of European thought, modern philosophy, and not enough out of tradition and scripture."

By the late 1970s and early 1980s, however, there were rumblings within the church hierarchy about the movement to transform the church of privilege in Latin America to the church of the poor. John Paul II began to express his misgivings about the influence of the Liberation Theology when radical priests and nuns became publicly associated with revolutionary efforts to overthrow established political systems. By the mid-1980s, the Vatican was silencing theologians and pulling the church back from involvement with the Liberation Theology in Latin America.

Because the base communities were set up in "opposition" to

the church in many places, they could not be ignored by the Vatican. And so the age-old internal conflict played itself out again between the Catholic church of vision and the Catholic church of operation. The church of vision included the papal encyclicals on work and human life, the social justice statements of the American Catholic bishops, and the whole tradition of Catholic social action. The church of operation, on the other hand, dealt with money, church practice, and the authority of the Pope and his bishops. As such, it was of paramount importance to Rome and the hierarchy, which presided over both "churches." Most Catholic theologians have had complete freedom to write and publish whatever they want for the church of vision, as long as they did not tread on doctrinal positions tied to the hierarchical authority of Rome. But when they began to question the standards of the church of operation, they most often got into trouble—and that is exactly what the Latin American theologians did.

"The base communities got into trouble because they claimed to be the church—thus, they waged an unwinable fight against an unbeatable foe," Cortes says.[10]

Cortes felt the IAF groups were fundamentally different from the base communities. "Theologically, we have always been in the mainstream of Catholic social thought," Cortes says. "Of course, we were challenged by what was going on in Latin America, but we were trying to develop a *North American* theology close to our own cultural experience. People who were drawn to the base communities saw them as separate from the local parish. They tended to disconnect from the church. We always wanted to work with the parish as an institution. It is important to us that what we do is connected to institutions, traditions, and history."

While the Catholic church backed away officially, the themes of Liberation Theology were taking hold among mainline American Protestant churches—mainly building on the insight that "evil is systematic."[11] Robert McAfee Brown, a social activist and Protestant theologian, became the leading advocate of Liberation Theology in the United States. Brown claimed that traditional Christianity had tended to "interpret evil in individualistic terms: a few bad people create the trouble, and if they can just be converted (or removed) all will be well."[12] Brown's message to Protestants was that, in order to fulfill the teachings of Jesus, they had an obligation to root out the systemic evils— to change society's institutions, to eliminate the causes of poverty and hunger.

It was not necessarily a new message for American Protestants. There had always been a strain of social activism in American Protestantism, producing that peculiar American brand of optimism and idealism that culminated in the 19th century abolitionist and suffrage movements. James Reichley, the author of *Religion in American Public Life,* believes that American Protestants, "far from denying the relevance of politics to religion, regarded social reform as the essence of the Christian message."[13]

From this early Protestant heritage came a set of ideas and political initiatives around the turn of the century that became known as the Social Gospel, set down in 1907 by a German-born Baptist minister, Walter Rauschenbusch. In *A Theology for the Social Gospel,* Rauschenbusch rejected the tendency of conservative evangelicals to identify sin with matters of personal behavior, such as drinking, dancing, cardplaying, or other turn-of-the-century "vices." For Rauschenbusch, the most important source of sin was not personal moral weakness, but an economic system than had "turned the patrimony of a nation into the private property of a small class."[14] The key concept of the Social Gospel was the pursuit of the Kingdom of God on earth, defined as the "realm of love" and the "commonwealth of labor." Both were believed to be achievable in human society. As such, the advocates of the Social Gospel, reformers rather than revolutionaries, worked to eliminate social evils such as sweatshops and rat-infested tenements, and they tried to create a physical environment where the "kingdom" might flourish. Actually, it was the ideas of the Social Gospel itself that flourished. They came to dominate Protestant seminaries of all denominations across the nation and helped create several generations of ministers and religious teachers who advocated its tenets. Under the influence of the Social Gospel, the Methodist Episcopal church adopted its first social creed in 1908. Other religious denominations followed suit, providing their members with calls to action in the political world to help create conditions that enhanced and complemented spiritual growth.

The legacy of the Social Gospel extended to the 1960s, with white Protestant involvement in the civil rights and antiwar movements developing from its remnants.

The excitement of the swirling ideas of the Liberation Theology and the old Social Gospel, coupled with the sense of frustration church activists felt over the failure of the Great Society's attempt to eliminate poverty and the despair over the American misadventure into Vietnam, created a fertile climate for the kinds of religious-based and values-laden organizing Cortes and the IAF were beginning to develop. Ministers, priests, and nuns recognized in the IAF organizing specific techniques to implement their deeply held religious and political values. For some, the Latin American *communidades de base* seemed to provide a model, and from what many church people were hearing about COPS or UNO, the IAF program appeared to be close to that model.

Although there are obvious similarities between the Christian base communities and the parish groups Cortes was training, he felt people were mistaken to look on them simply as a derivative. The IAF groups, COPS in San Antonio, UNO in Los Angeles, and the dozen or so groups that came later, never had as their central purpose a revolutionary critique of the government or church structures. In COPS, the religious dimension itself was almost a by-product of the organizing, the result of the personal interests of Cortes and key leaders, rather than part of a grand theological strategy. Although composed of church-based memberships, the local groups were never part of any church hierarchy. They were always independent and becoming more ecumenical and less Catholic as time went on. The IAF groups also arose out of a strong democratic tradition, encompassing the philosophy of Thomas Jefferson, the values of populism, and the tactics of Saul Alinsky, as well as the practical experience of almost 50 years of community organizing. The Latin American base communities developed from an entirely different tradition—under Third World social and economic conditions in which democracy was most often a remote dream and extreme poverty a daily reality. The calls to action by liberation theologians were almost desperate, reflecting the tensions of a feudal culture in the modern age.

Cortes and the IAF, an amalgam of ideas from many sources,

did selectively borrow from the liberation theologians—particularly from Freire's ideas on education and development of the "whole" individual. The emphasis on the growth and development of people through dialogue with others and the development of a sense of "personhood" within a supportive community were undoubtedly shaped by the ideas of the Catholic theologians—just as they were shaped by close readings of modern psychology and philosophers like Hannah Arendt, as well as early Christian history, which detailed the development of the close-knit communities that created the early church.

It is a long circuitous route from the first century Christian communities to the *communidades de base* to parish meetings in San Antonio or East Los Angeles. But a faint trail is there, and the scent of that trail began to attract hundreds of people whose religious beliefs led them to seek an outlet for involvement in their communities. But it was not only Catholics who were affected. In 1978, Protestants joined Catholics in calling Cortes back to Texas to organize.

13

We Are Not an Illusion
of the Moment

Houston, 1978

Houston, Texas, is a city true to its past.

It grew out of a land development scheme in a hot, humid, mosquito-infested marsh in 1836 when two imaginative entrepreneurs—J.K. and A.C. Allen—persuaded Texas hero Sam Houston to lend his name to the settlement in return for a few acres of free land. Sam Houston also used his influence in 1837 to help the outpost become the capital of the new Republic of Texas.[1] In the next two years, the city's population tripled from 500 to 1,500, and the Allen brothers began to make a fortune. With Sam Houston on their side, the developers boasted to their East Coast investors that their city would soon become the "great commercial emporium of Texas."[2]

For the next 142 years, other imaginative developers, cotton brokers, merchants, railroaders, bankers, oil producers, shippers, and lawyers had a host of public officials on their side as well, and they made deals every bit as clever as the Allen brothers' alliance with Sam Houston. Like the Allens, their money-making schemes helped the city grow.

With access to the waterways that led to the Gulf of Mexico only 50 miles away, as well as the proximity of rich timber, cotton, and oil of the East Texas fields, Houston attracted ambitious men who understood that the city could become a center for trade and marketing. Each generation of business leaders learned how to use public money, not just public names, to finance their dreams—larger than anything the Allen brothers had ever imagined. First, they wanted deep-water sea ports and commercial rail and highway transportation networks. Then, it was rights-of-way for oil pipelines and legislation to protect private utility conglomerates and publicly financed, but privately managed, water systems. Later, they went after the U.S. Space Center and even built the first domed sports stadium in the United States—the Astrodome. With their money and power, they persuaded or elected mayors, governors, congressmen—even presidents—to approve financing schemes that put hundreds of millions of tax dollars into their projects. And the public money also helped lure private investors, sometimes through advertisements in the *New York Times*—like the one as far back as 1909, which explained that Houston was so hospitable to business development that "her city hall is a business house."[3]

By 1978, the efforts of these men, plus rising oil prices and a hot Sun Belt business climate, had produced a city of 1.6 million people. Houston was home to the nation's premier petrochemical complex; the second largest sea port in the nation; huge centers of banking, utilities, and medical research; glistening glass skyscrapers; world-class museums and symphony halls; and more than 1,700 square miles of residential developments whose houses were made habitable only by the hum of air conditioning units that operated at least 10 months of the year.[4]

When Ernie Cortes arrived in Houston in 1978, he knew that it was different from anything he had seen in San Antonio and East Los Angeles. The city was controlled by the natural heirs to the old "Suite 8F Crowd," a group of powerful business leaders who in the 1930s began to gather regularly for drinks in Suite 8F of the old Lamar Hotel.[5] The modern business entrepreneurs who now ran Houston—downtown real estate developers, bankers, and corporate leaders—had learned from Suite 8F's master builders how to fight for what they cared about, and since the 1830s, what Houston leaders had cared about most was *making money*. Government's role was to assist them or get out of the way, which Houston's city and county governments obligingly did—with publicly financed infrastructure projects, low business taxes, and no zoning regulations to control development. Because the business community and people they elected decided how to allocate public resources, Houston's city government provided paltry public services, and its public schools were notoriously underfunded, several times facing loss of state accreditation for failure to meet minimum standards. Houston had inadequate public housing, primitive welfare services, and overextended religious and private charities that struggled to provide help for the people who fell through the cracks of the city's general prosperity. And there were cracks.

Boomtown Houston in 1978 had pockets of urban poverty as devastating as Watts or Harlem. Almost 20 percent of its population was black, and many people lived in run-down inner-city areas, like the Fifth Ward, that were basically ignored as the city expanded outward into sprawling white suburbs. Houston's blacks were in a recession even when the city was booming, with black unemployment at times as high as 25 percent in the late 1970s.[6] The plight of Houston's blacks, as well as a generally impoverished Hispanic population swollen by new immigrants from Mexico and Central America, plus the tightly controlled power at the city hall "business house," led local churches to invite Ernie Cortes to begin organizing.

The Metropolitan Ministries, a private ecumenical social services agency dominated by Presbyterian, Lutheran, and Episcopalian ministers, enthusiastically promoted an Industrial Areas Foundation organizing effort as early as 1976.[7] They had heard about COPS and how its political power had shifted tax money to poor areas of San Antonio and created a well-trained army of community leaders who stood up for their neighbors and neighborhoods. They wanted the same for Houston. So they created an organizing committee and hired as coordinator 25-year-old Robert Rivera, a former VISTA volunteer who could match Ernie Cortes in both enthusiasm and bulk. They also came up with a name, The Metropolitan Organization, TMO, reflecting the city-wide ecumenical and interracial nature of the organization they hoped to build. The ministers knew that for all of its flamboyance, Houston was still grounded in southern Protestant traditions, and if a new organization were to succeed, it could not rely solely on Catholics, as had COPS. Instead, it would have to have a base of Protestant churches at its core.

Yet the Catholics, too, wanted to be involved in Houston. Cortes recalls that in 1976, Houston priest John McCarthy, later to become bishop of the Catholic diocese in Austin, was so impressed with COPS that he kept urging Cortes to get something similar going in Houston. Once, at McCarthy's suggestion, Cortes and IAF director Ed Chambers drove aimlessly around Houston looking at the city and trying to imagine how they could organize it. "Then we met with McCarthy in a 'socks-off' kind of meeting where we drank scotch and talked about our dreams," Cortes says. "What appealed to McCarthy was the feeling that our organizing was what social justice was all about. He thought it was important for the church to be involved." So, with McCarthy's backing and the support of Father Joseph Fiorenza, who was then chancellor of the Houston-Galveston Diocese and later its bishop, Cortes began to steal time away from COPS to join Ed Chambers for exploratory meetings in Houston with both Protestants and Catholics. But then Cortes decided to move to Los Angeles, and Chambers sent an IAF-trained organizer, Peter Martinez, to continue meeting with Houston ministers. However, no more than a dozen or so exploratory meetings had been held in Houston in 1976 before the effort fizzled.

One of the early participants in the TMO meetings had been alarmed by the Alinsky-IAF connection and had gone to the Houston newspapers to warn about the "outside agitators" who were coming to Houston to stir up poor people. A critical newspaper article, dredging up the IAF's role in the 1965 fight with Kodak in Rochester, scared away some of the Protestants, and the early effort failed. A former mayor of Houston, businessman Louis Welch, was plainly contemptuous of the involvement of Houston churches in a political effort, telling one leader that "the only thing churches are capable of running are school buses and they don't do that very well."[8]

"Even though everything was a shambles in Houston, Robert Rivera was still excited about it," Cortes says. But Rivera had decided to become an IAF organizer, and he went to San Antonio for training with COPS. Before he left, however, he and others persuaded Sister Christine Stephens to become chair of a sponsoring committee to keep hope for the effort alive. Stephens, who split her time between running a local parish social services office and managing the Campaign for Human Development for the diocese, spent the next two years recruiting pastors and raising money. By 1978, she had put together a coalition of 32 churches and $200,000. TMO formally invited Cortes to come back to Texas to organize full-time in Houston. And Ernie Cortes was eager to come.

"I wanted to organize in Houston more than any other place in Texas," Cortes says. He also wanted to return to Texas from California, particularly since he had remarried and settled into a comfortable domestic life with Oralia Garza. Slight and delicate, serious and smart, Garza had once worked for a Cortes-led voter registration project in San Antonio. Active in community politics, she was as committed to the organizing effort as Cortes, providing from her observations and experience keen personal insights that complemented Cortes' political instincts. For Cortes, Oralia Garza also offered a balance that anchored him in the family values he had been espousing in San Antonio and Los Angeles. It was an anchor he particularly needed for this new organizing effort in Houston. From the beginning, there were problems.

Houston was simply too big. Its minority populations were scattered in enclaves throughout the city, isolated from each other and difficult to penetrate. The rapid growth of the 1960s and early 1970s created neighborhoods in transition, with very little feeling of "community" among residents. The city's newspaper rarely focused on neighborhood needs or poverty in the midst of plenty, so there was a sense that neighborhood problems—where they existed—were simply aberrations. Houston also had no tradition of "fighting city hall," and it was hard to convince people that they might be successful with their localized efforts, much less anything city-wide. The local black and Hispanic political leadership concentrated its efforts on selected congressional and legislative districts where their numbers could ensure victories. Complicating matters further was the fact that many of the area's blue-collar whites worked in unionized industries where the wages were relatively high and where motivation for solidarity with the minority working poor was relatively low. There was also little connection between blacks and Hispanics. In fact, there was suspicion, and sometimes even hostility.

When the Reverend Robert McGee, a black Methodist minister, first heard about TMO, he thought it was another COPS—an all-Catholic, Hispanic organization. "At first, I didn't see how it was going to benefit us," he said. So McGee and other black ministers in Houston took a wait-and-see attitude. "We decided that if they did some good things, then we'd come on board."[9]

It was a catch-22 situation. TMO couldn't be successful with its target audience—the black community—unless it had the support of the ministers and churches, and it couldn't get that support until it was successful. Many of the black ministers Cortes was trying to recruit were concerned that TMO would disrupt their alliances with local politicians and officeholders. Although those alliances had rarely generated any lasting social change, they could at least provide critical assistance when a minister really needed it—to get someone out of jail or find a job for a friend at city hall. As such, the problem for Cortes was not so much to persuade pastors of the need to get involved politically; many of them *were* involved. The task for Cortes was to convince the ministers that there was a different and better method to engage in politics—one that would not let politicians off the hook with election-eve visits to black churches, or street money on election day, or a few token jobs for black activists.

Sister Christine Stephens, who cut her political teeth on the Houston organizing effort as chair of the sponsoring committee, said the task was to "redo the political culture. . . . You have people who set themselves up as brokers. So when you form an organization . . . you're really trying to break that broker system, saying there's no one person . . . who brokers that community. . . . You're trying to change the people's way of thinking about politics so they will be involved in the political process on a much more regular basis, not just voting."[10]

So Ernie Cortes, and the church leaders who brought him to Houston, began the slow, tedious process of defining a new political culture that would allow neighborhood people to become directly involved in the decision-making that affected them—without going through someone else. It took months of one-on-one sessions, house meetings, parish development, and leader training before it began to sink in.

Rev. McGee gradually began to see the value of the new kind of political organization the TMO sponsoring committee was trying to establish and how it could be a vehicle for the "Lord's work" in the community. "We just had to get people to begin assuming some responsibility and ownership in the community," he said. "Our churches had to be more than places to worship and go home to feel good. People had to go home and help God assume responsibility."

TMO began to appeal to other black leaders as well. "I come from a background of working with the NAACP and other movement-type organizations," said Michael Jackson, a young TMO leader. "Within TMO there is a strong emphasis on educating the individuals to be more responsible for themselves. This was quite different from other work I'd done."[11]

It was different, and the process was exceedingly slow. Once again, as in 1976, after only one or two small-scale meetings between some TMO members and city hall functionaries, word got out that some of Houston's disenchanted citizens were organizing outside of normal political channels. The news alarmed some of the city's business leaders. A few of them began calling on ministers and priests of TMO member churches, threatening to withhold their contributions if the church-supported community organizing continued. They started with the Catholics, with whom they had substantial financial leverage.

An ex-CIA agent organized parishioners against TMO in St. Jerome's parish. When Father Joseph Fiorenza, then the chancellor of the diocese, visited the parish, he was booed by church members because of his support of TMO. Even the bishop of the Houston-Galveston Diocese at that time, the late John Markovsky, felt the heat directly. One of the most wealthy and prominent Catholics in his diocese, George Strake, who would later become Texas secretary of state and chairman of the state Republican party, urged Markovsky to drop his support of TMO. But the bishop went "toe-to-toe with him and held firm," according to Richard Daly, executive director of the Texas Catholic Conference, the social action arm of Texas' Catholic bishops.[12] Although Bishop Markovsky was known as a religious and political conservative, he held fast to the church's teachings that recognized the right of poor people and workers to organize to better their lives, and he followed those teachings with regard to TMO. His support for the organization never wavered—and that support became essential.[13] It kept Catholic parishes in the organizing loop, and it gave priests, nuns, and even Protestant ministers courage to stay with the project. But even more importantly, it gave TMO what it most needed to survive: time. With Catholic support and more black Protestant ministers coming on board, Cortes had the chance to develop his intensive internal training programs. He was able to produce a core group of committed leaders—white, black, and Hispanic—who developed their political skills through neighborhood actions and small improvements: a stop sign at a dangerous intersection, an after-school program for children of working parents, storm drains to stop localized flooding, old-fashioned police foot-patrols to cut crime in the black Fifth Ward—the kinds of minor victories that gave TMO's new leaders the chance to learn the Iron Rule and develop some measure of self-confidence and public experience.

TMO leaders learned to spot key issues that provided just enough grist to grind the interest of the growing numbers of new recruits—high electric bills, inadequate public transportation, drugs in the schools. Five hundred people would show up for a meeting here, a thousand for a meeting there.

"They thought they had killed us in Houston, but here we'd come again," Cortes says.

TMO was beginning to influence inner-city voter turnout and election results in about 100 of the 600-plus precincts in the county, which was enough to get politicians to notice, particularly within some of Houston's city council districts. TMO neighborhood groups began to have regular meetings with certain council members—even with Houston's police chief. The training and small successful encounters over the years began to pay off. Although TMO's successes did not generate the sparks or sparkle of COPS in San Antonio, they did create a stable, sustaining membership base that grew to 60 local congregations representing about 75,000 families.

That base began to give TMO serious clout by the early 1980s, when the organization finally got city government to put its first restrictions on development—a historic break with the past.

When the Almeda shopping mall was built in southeast Houston in the late 1970s, nearby residential neighborhoods immediately experienced an increase in flooding after heavy rains. Because Houston had no zoning regulations, nothing prevented the mall's developers from building on a flood plain, and nothing required them to provide for the increase runoff resulting from paving over miles of pervious cover. Going to bat for the neighborhoods, TMO consulted with water and construction engineers and put together a presentation for the city council that called for a building moratorium in the area. But the idea of *any* restriction on development was anathema at city hall, and administrators would not even admit that there was a relationship between building and flooding.

"TMO was the first organization in Houston to point out to the city that the building of retention ponds in parking lots could reduce the rate of runoff after rains to keep from over-loading the drainage system and flooding the area," Sister Christine Stephens recalls. "For Houston—this developer bo-nanza—it was unheard of to require any preventative mea-sures."

TMO argued that the developers, as well as the city, had a responsibility to plan for the consequences of their activities. When TMO presented its voluminous research, backed up with dozens of meetings between neighborhood leaders and public officials, the argument began to sink in, first at the county level and then at city hall.

"We didn't get a total building moratorium, but we did get a localized watershed moratorium in the southeast," Stephens explains. "This meant that developers couldn't build anything that would cause *more* runoff than already existed. They would have to build flood retention ponds and other devices to con-trol flooding. In three years, this became a city-wide policy, and we had created a major change in Houston's attitude toward development."

The Houston organizing project was significant to the IAF not just for these kinds of victories and the ability to survive under attack. It was also important because of the bonus emer-gence of two strong leaders who decided to become full-time

IAF organizers. Houston produced first Robert Rivera—a smart, stocky scrounger for new recruits, a quick learner with an instinct for political action, who was as tenacious in his approach to organizing as an 18-wheeler climbing a mountain highway: he believed he could make it even when others had doubts. Later, Sister Christine Stephens decided to become a full-time organizer and brought her maturity, feminist sensibility, and convent respectability to the effort. The presence of Rivera and Stephens gave Ernie Cortes the time to move around Texas in response to appeals to set up COPS-like organizations in Fort Worth, the Rio Grande Valley, El Paso, Austin, and other cities. It also gave him colleagues to work with and see regularly. And more importantly, it gave him time to reflect on the pluralistic organizations emerging under his guidance.

When Protestants began to be involved in Houston and the other organizations Cortes was initiating in Texas, an internal tension rarely present in COPS appeared. Cortes believes it was a "creative" tension, however, because it encouraged the examination of basic doctrines of many faiths to find common kernels of truth. But the Protestant and Catholic differences sometimes made the tactics of organizing more difficult.

Once, when Cortes was trying to get a group of middle-class white Protestants to narrow their range of issues and focus on what was really important to them, he told the group, "You've got to know what you want, you've got to have something that you want bad enough to kick and scream and claw about, even to act *im-po-lite-ly* about." He slowly emphasized each syllable so that the word and its meaning would sink in.[14]

"Ah, but Ernie," a Presbyterian minister laughingly interrupted. "We like to approach this in a more intellectual fashion. We like to reason together, to debate the issues and argue politely. We don't like to yell and scream."

"That's right," Cortes retorted. "The politicians think only the rag-tag Mexican Catholics and black Baptists will yell at them . . . so they don't worry about you. But it is important for them to see your anger. It means you're ready to fight."

Cortes believes that their discomfort with anger is one of the reasons it was harder initially to get Protestants in Houston and elsewhere involved in the kinds of actions that made COPS famous. But it is not the only reason. "They're not used to doing things together," Cortes says of the Protestants. "Sometimes we want everyone to stand up at the same time or to speak out in unison, or to walk out together. It's awkward for them because they're not used to acting together as are the Catholics."

Yet the mix of diverse cultures and religions produced its moments of feeling and ferment. "There is a tremendous dynamic which goes on when you mix middle class and poor, black, white, and Hispanic," Ed Chambers believes. "The excitement comes in the process of working out the tension."

Patricia Ozuna, a San Antonio COPS leaders, agrees. A Catholic, Ozuna told of a moving experience for her with Protestant members within the emerging network of Texas organizations. "Several of our organizations were looking for a way to come together to build a common experience," she said. "The executive leadership came up with the idea to get leaders from each organization to come together and share a Bible verse that inspired them to help others in the community. At the meeting, people read to each other from their Bibles."[15]

One member chose a passage from the first epistle of John: "But if a man has enough to live on, and yet when he sees his brother in need shuts up his heart against him, how can it be said that the divine love dwells in him? My children, love must not be a matter of words or talk; it must be genuine and show itself in action" (I John 3:17–18).

Another picked a verse from Isaiah: "This, rather is the fasting that I wish: releasing those bound unjustly, untying the thongs of the yoke; setting free the oppressed, breaking every yoke" (Isaiah 58:6).

And someone chose the familiar words from Matthew: "Truly, I say to you, as you did it to one of the least of these, my brethren, you did it to me" (Matthew 25:40).

As Ozuna described the Hispanic Catholics, black Baptists, and white Methodists and Unitarians reading passages of the Bible that meant something to them, her voice cracked with emotion. "Here were people who had a wide difference in income. The voices were different, the religions had their differences, but the words were the same," Ozuna said. "There was a common message that united them. It still gives me goose bumps."

To Ernie Cortes, Ed Chambers, and the thousands of TMO members who stayed involved in the organization even though it never received the kind of acclaim that surrounded COPS, this process was "where the action is." According to Chambers, "A community-dynamic church is what is being formed. You leave people in their individual denominations, but you come together for self-interest, for social action. You build around the central values which people will act on."

The process, he believes, is as beneficial to the churches as to the church leaders who transform themselves into politicians. "You've got to keep the Catholic and Protestant churches honest," Chambers says. "If left to themselves, they'll get righteous about being Christians with all those clean unadulterated values. They'll say, 'we are right and everyone else is wrong.' You need the diversity of our organizations to keep people accountable. Without it, we'd only be building a working-class Christian political party."

While the emerging IAF organizations in Texas had no desire to become a working-class Christian political party, they also did not want to be considered one more pitiable "romantic" grass-roots organization, according to Father A. Murphy, a black Episcopal priest from Los Angeles who is one of the few Protestants active in the United Neighborhoods Organization. Speaking at COPS' 10th anniversary convention, which also included representatives from TMO and other new Texas IAF organizations, Murphy said, "We will not settle for the trappings of power. We are not a rainbow coalition . . . an illusion of the moment. . . . We are about the business of witnessing the seeds of black, brown and white political power."[16]

In Houston, the Texas IAF began its first mass planting of those seeds.

Part Four

*Behold, I am doing a rare thing; now
it springs forth, do you not perceive it?*

Isaiah 44:19

14

Is COPS Coming
to Your Neighborhood?

New York, 1986

Texas Lieutenant Governor William P. Hobby Jr. and I share a cab to La Guardia Airport on a crisp fall afternoon. It is one of those interminable rides out of Manhattan, with the mix of high speed, quick stops, and long waits that sends most Texans in New York into orbit. But I am relatively free of anxiety because we have plenty of time before our plane departs and Hobby is calm because . . . Hobby is always calm, sometimes even maddeningly so.

We have been in New York to see the bond rating agencies about the financial condition of the State of Texas, which has not been good since the price of oil slipped from $21 to $11 a barrel. Wall Street is wary of Texas' ability to meet its obligations, and we have been part of a delegation to reassure investment bankers and bond analysts that state officials will behave responsibly and with fiscal "prudence." No one in the state can do a better job of reassuring Wall Street than quiet, serious— even shy—Bill Hobby, who since 1972 has stood guard against extremism in Texas government.

Under Texas' weak executive form of government, the lieutenant governor, through his powers over the state senate, controls the flow of legislation, state spending, and even the governor's executive appointments, which the senate must confirm. Traditionally, Texas' lieutenant governors have wielded more power than the governor, and Hobby has become one of the all-time masters of the system—not by any blustery good-old-boy bravado, but through a low-key, consensus-building style. He has extended the protective arm of his office over people whose loyalty could be counted on when it mattered—from ego-driven state senators whom he rarely made vote on issues that could defeat them in their districts, to opportunistic agency officials whom he selectively allowed into his inner circle. In the process, he protected the financial interests of Texas' biggest businesses while shielding basic education and health and welfare services from some of the state's more reactionary anti-taxers and budget-cutters. Bill Hobby is unquestionably the most powerful state officeholder in Texas. He is also the best friend Ernie Cortes and his network of church organizations have in state government.

"It's interesting that the politician who understands us best is rather conservative," Sister Christine Stephens once said of Hobby. "Someone who is a thinking conservative like Hobby can understand what it is we're trying to do because they more often deal in the real world, without always dealing in the future world or looking at the impact on the future of actions now."

I try to take advantage of our time in the real-world New York traffic to ask Hobby what he really thinks about Cortes and his organizations. But a conversation with Hobby is slow-paced. This "thinking conservative" takes time to ponder my questions. He sits silently and looks out of the window, and I worry that he has forgotten my question—and me—sitting inches away from him in the back seat of this taxi.

Finally, after clearing his throat several times, he begins speaking. "I agree with what they're doing. It's simple. If you don't want to see sewage running in the streets, then you've got to be for them."[1]

Hobby was the first major politician Cortes took into the South Texas *colonias,* and he was so appalled by what he saw that he vowed to do something about it. Once, in front of 5,000 people and a galaxy of news reporters who were eager to record a confrontational "accountability" session, Hobby give a proud and resounding "yes" when Valley Interfaith leaders asked him point blank, "Are you willing to commit $100 million to bring water, sewer lines, and paved roads to families living in the Rio Grande Valley *colonias?*" Hobby's staff members later said that although Hobby had no idea where he would get the money, he got so caught up in the spirit of the rally that he decided he just had to commit state funds to these people. Afterward, his staff frantically tried to find the money to fulfill their boss's commitment.

"I've never been uncomfortable with their 'pinnings' and 'accountability' sessions," Hobby tells me as he laughingly describes a state senator who ran away every time he saw any of the Industrial Areas Foundation people approaching. Hobby is amused because one of former Governor Mark White's press aides raised hell with him every time the governor's office had to deal with Cortes—as if Hobby himself were responsible for him, which he is not, although Hobby obviously enjoys the rapport with Cortes, as well as the perception that they are friends.

Hobby's appreciation for Cortes began as early as 1972, the first time he was running for the office of lieutenant governor. Hobby said San Antonio was a "mess" that year, and Cortes provided Hobby's aides a road map to the Byzantine world of its politics. But not until the battle for statewide education reform, led by billionaire Ross Perot, did Hobby really come to know Cortes. In 1984, the legislature overhauled public education—reducing classroom size, requiring teacher competency testing, creating the "no pass/no play" rules for extracurricular activities, and, most importantly, redistributing state funds among the 1,200 school districts so that poor local districts received a greater share of the state's money.

"Ross Perot is generally given credit for Texas' education reforms. But it could not have happened without Ernie's groups," said Hobby. "That was quite a team—the nuns, Cortes, and H. Ross Perot!"[2]

Hobby's staff members say that what the lieutenant governor admires most about Cortes and his groups is that they do what they say they will do—and do it well. Hobby's top aide, Saralee Tiede, who had 20 years experience as a news reporter covering the capital before going to work for Hobby, said she and Hobby were impressed with the way Cortes educated his people. "They put out a book on school finance that was the best thing I've ever seen. It made the complexities of the issues understandable to anyone," Teide said.[3] Hobby's admiration for Cortes is also shaped by awe for his erudition. "I'm amazed at the intellect of Ernie, his widespread interests and reading habits," Hobby says.

The Hobby-Cortes relationship has been crucial to the development of political power for the IAF network of organizations in Texas. And the Catholic bishops of the state initially paved the way for its development. Richard Daly, the college professor and Holy Cross brother who serves as the lobbyist for Texas' 14 Catholic bishops, recounts that one of Hobby's staff members called him in 1982 to find out how the bishops felt about Ernie Cortes and The Metropolitan Organization in Houston, Hobby's hometown. Hobby was considering appearing at a TMO accountability session, along with his Republican opponent in the 1982 election, George Strake.

"All Hobby wanted to know was did Ernie really have the support of the bishops," Daly said. "When I told him 'yes,' Hobby decided to go to the meeting."[4]

As it turned out, Hobby's appearance at the TMO meeting proved to be fortuitous for the establishment of the IAF organizational network in Texas. Because it was an election year, Hobby's advisers were beginning to see the voting potential of Cortes' groups. They realized that in a close election, those votes might make a significant difference, particularly in San Antonio, which a Democratic candidate needed to carry to win statewide. A COPS-led get-out-the-vote drive could generate more than 50,000 West Side votes, and that could be critical in the upcoming November election. Hobby was concerned about his reelection campaign because he was facing the first serious challenge to his office since he had been elected 10 years earlier.

Bill Hobby had come to Texas politics with a pedigree few could match. His father had been governor of Texas in the 1920s, and his mother, Oveta Culp Hobby, headed the WACS in World War II and went on to serve in President Eisenhower's cabinet as the first head of the Department of Health, Education, and Welfare. Until 1987, the family owned the *Houston Post* and represented establishment Texas at its best—moderately conservative, socially responsible, and righteously reasonable. But ideologically pure Texas Republicans were no longer leaving it up to conservative Democrats like Hobby to carry their banner. They picked another wealthy scion of the Texas establishment to oppose Hobby—lean, prep-school–handsome oilman George Strake, who had a tight grip on the Texas GOP'S right wing.

Ironically, it had been Strake who had tried to persuade Catholic Bishop Markovsky to pull the plug on TMO in Houston in 1976. Although unsuccessful with the bishop, Strake had spent years toiling to build a vital Republican party in Texas. His efforts in 1978 helped elect Bill Clements the first Republican governor of Texas since Reconstruction, and Clements had appointed Strake his secretary of state, giving him statewide exposure. With Strake as his running mate for lieutenant governor in 1982, Governor Clements was being challenged in his reelection bid by Democratic Attorney General Mark White. That meant that the Republicans would pull out all the stops to save Clements and beat Hobby as well.

To survive a Republican gubernatorial onslaught, Hobby had to generate enthusiasm for his own candidacy among the liberal wing of the Democratic party—not always easy for a politician of Hobby's stripe. But every action Hobby could take to increase the voter turnout among traditional Democratic voters—particularly Hispanic and black voters who gave Democrats from 60 to 95 percent of their votes in some areas—would help his cause. Hobby needed to reach the very people TMO and COPS represented. But he wanted some assurance that TMO was not just another noisy political organization without the resources to match its rhetoric.

When Richard Daly, speaking for the Catholic bishops, gave Hobby that assurance, Hobby decided to attend TMO's rally even though Ernie Cortes made it clear to him that he could expect no formal endorsement from the nonpartisan group.

The Houston event drew about 1,000 TMO members, and Hobby—who is often an awkward public speaker—expertly answered TMO's questions, whereas his opponent stumbled and allowed his antipathy for the group to derail rational responses to their questions.

"Hobby did so well at the meeting that his staff was ecstatic,"

Cortes says. "A few days later, Hobby came off the victor in a statewide television debate with Strake, and his staff felt that it was due to the boost of confidence he got from the accountability session with TMO. After the Houston experience, Hobby was willing to do anything for the network."

Cortes knew exactly what he wanted Hobby to do: come to El Paso. It sounded simple enough, and Hobby agreed to speak to a rally put together by Cortes' new organization there—with the hope that he would benefit from COPS' nonpartisan get-out-the-vote drive on the West Side of San Antonio for the November election.

What Hobby did not know at the time was that war was being waged in El Paso against the network's fledgling organization, the El Paso Interreligious Sponsoring Committee—EPISO. If something were not done soon, EPISO would surely lose the war and become mired in the same kind of organizing swamp that had almost sunk TMO in Houston.

"We were being attacked viscously by the right-wing," according to Robert Rivera, who in 1982 had taken on the chief organizing duties in El Paso, where Hispanics constituted almost 70 percent of the city's 480,000 residents. "There was selective harassment of our leaders, myself, of any politician who would meet with us. Sometimes 50 people would show up at our meetings and disrupt things. They distributed pink leaflets calling us Stalinists, and there was something negative in the media about us almost everyday."[5]

Conservative Catholic church members who opposed the Liberation Theology and feared the growing influence of the IAF in Texas had organized a group called "EPISO No, Christo Si." Some had infiltrated the parish groups affiliated with EPISO. Even the IAF's Ed Chambers unwittingly contributed to the problem by telling an El Paso newspaper reporter, somewhat tongue-in-cheek, that the IAF organizers were troublemakers, that their "job was to cause trouble." The problem was compounded when an El Paso television station picked up a news feature series, originally produced in San Antonio and received favorably there, called "Is COPS Coming to Your Neighborhood?" But when it ran in El Paso, "it evoked a kind of mindless fear," according to Rivera. Protestant church members began to back away. Only the United Methodists and the Catholic bishop remained supportive.

Larry McNeil, a full-time organizer and member of the IAF cabinet, remembers being met at the El Paso airport by a newspaper reporter who was developing a story about IAF organizing there. McNeil says he was asked point blank, "Are you a socialist or Communist?"[6] McNeil, a native of deep East Texas, a Southern Baptist, and a former Vanderbilt seminarian, tried to laugh it off. He understood that as an "outsider" he was a convenient target for anyone opposed to the changes IAF organizations bring to a community. Attacks on "outside agitators" had always formed a pattern of opposition to IAF organizing. And Saul Alinsky's controversial reputation didn't help. "Alinsky-type radical" was spit out like a single-word epithet whenever IAF organizers came around, having the same effect in some quarters as saying "this room is full of rats." One El Paso Baptist minister said he feared "East Coast communists were trying to run his town."[7]

Cortes reacted angrily to these kinds of charges, once tearing into a reporter who brought up the issue: "Are you going to tell me that chief executives of every corporation in this state were all born in Texas? People are always bringing in outside help. When rich people hire agitators they call them consultants or strategic planners. But when poor people try to do it, there's something wrong."

The real fear about IAF organizing Cortes believes "was about organizing workers . . . particularly in the Valley and El Paso. They look at all those Mexicans and realize that if somebody organizes them into unions, it's all over. It's an economic question in the long run," he asserts.

But the opposition to IAF organizing was also mired in Catholic church politics, because those most opposed were Catholics deeply upset with their church after Vatican II. Conservative church members didn't like the changes in the liturgy, the increasing social activism of priests and nuns, and the emphasis on the needs of society rather than on the needs of the soul. But the Catholic opposition in El Paso had the unexpected effect of driving the Protestants away.

"We wanted a broad base—more than just Mexicans," Cortes

says. "We were organizing in the Anglo community as well. But after the attacks, these people just fled like the disciples after Gethsemene."

Cortes and organizer Rivera were particularly stunned when Episcopal Bishop Richard Trelease reneged on a pledge of $25,000 to support EPISO after 25 prominent Episcopalians turned up at a meeting to protest the church pledge. The bishop explained to Rivera that there was not a single person at the meeting in favor of his support of EPISO, and later in a personal letter to Rivera, the bishop told him that although he admired what Rivera and EPISO were trying to do, he was sorry that Rivera still did not understand "the policy of the Episcopal Church and my forced withdrawal from EPISO."[8]

Hobby received a flood of calls from his supporters in El Paso who were concerned about his public association with EPISO. But Hobby ignored their warnings. He had given his word. And because Hobby was to attend, El Paso's mayor and other elected officials who had ignored EPISO earlier also felt it would be safe to be associated with the group. They agreed to join Hobby on stage for the event.

The rally was a tremendous success—more than 1,500 people attended.

It was a typical IAF mass gathering—well organized, colorful, on schedule, and run with almost a military precision that had been perfected by COPS leaders over the years. Whole church groups sat together under banners proclaiming their parish names and neighborhoods. Floor leaders wore identifying arm bands and gave instructions to EPISO members on when to stand or applaud or be silent. There was music and singing, bright banners, American flags and balloons, as well as prominently displayed blowups of biblical quotations. Several generations of families attended together—grandmothers holding small children, men and women dressed in their Sunday best. Ministers, priests, and nuns were a visible presence in the crowd. EPISO leaders were on the stage with the politicians, maintaining control and running the meeting, telling the politicians—including Hobby—when to talk, sit down, or be quiet. The television crews and newspaper reporters who covered the rally were obviously impressed, and their stories reflected the beginning of new respect for EPISO.

"The right-wing was just not given the same credibility after the rally," Rivera said. The press stopped covering the anti-EPISO protesters. The crisis was over. And EPISO at last began to concentrate on developing leaders, recruiting new churches, and increasing Hispanic voter registration, which in 1983 was only 37 percent of its potential.

"We were fighting for survival," Rivera said. "If it hadn't been for the lieutenant governor coming to El Paso, there probably wouldn't even be an organization there. He doesn't know this, but he was instrumental in our survival . . . he didn't understand the urgency of our invitation to speak, but he agreed to go because he was worried about his own reelection."

Through a well-financed "unity" effort, Hobby and all the Democrats won the election in November, throwing out Republican Governor Clements and bringing into office fresh new faces to Texas state government.[9] With Hobby's reelection, the relationship of the powerful legislative leader with Cortes was cemented. Hobby had proved to Cortes that he was a man of his word. He kept his commitment to speak in El Paso even after some of his closest supporters advised him to cancel. And the Cortes organizations proved to Hobby that they could deliver votes. The 1982 vote in San Antonio was overwhelmingly Democratic, and Mexican-American voters statewide gave Hobby 88 percent of their vote.

The alliance between Hobby and Cortes gave poor and middle-class church people access to power at the executive level in Texas. They used it in the 1984 legislative session not only to influence the public school reform debate, but to help enact an indigent health-care program that extended medical treatment to more than 200,000 poor Texas women and children. The presence of the IAF groups in the state capital was hard to ignore—from their rallies of 10,000 people on the Capitol grounds to groups of 10 and 20 local IAF leaders patrolling the halls of the state house to catch key legislative leaders. The self-assurance and firm resolve of the IAF leaders threw old-time legislators, lobbyists, and staff off guard. The IAF leaders were not like the other groups of poor people who occasionally came to call. COPS members from San Antonio who had been studying school finance issues for six years carried around thick notebooks full of data on school funding plans. They were formidable, as was Cortes.

"Cortes is so tough, he makes nails look soft," one lobbyist said. A legislator agreed. "You don't want to have those people on your tail for any reason." Others complained that when they agreed to a meeting with Cortes, they would be stunned when he showed up with 10 or 15 people who crowded into tiny legislative offices to talk about specific and technical provisions of the state's education code. One key Hispanic leader thought a lot of the meetings were simply unnecessary. "They call you to meet them for breakfast at 8 A.M. on a Saturday morning and things like that. It seems more like a test of loyalty to them than anything else," he said.

Saralee Tiede, the former news reporter turned Hobby aide, complained that working with Valley Interfaith leaders on a tour of the *colonias* was "one of the most exasperating things I've done. They wanted control of the whole trip, insisted on being listed as sponsors, had to take credit for everything. It was all or nothing with them. Without total control, they didn't want to participate," she charged. Tiede admits that she may not have always understood their goals. "I thought they wanted change and lasting power, but sometimes it looked more like a big ego trip."

But Stan Schleuter, the conservative former Texas legislator who headed the committee that had to pass a $1 billion tax bill to pay for the education reforms, lauded the IAF groups' repeated trips to Austin to support both school reform and the new taxes to pay for it. "That took courage," he said.[10] Computer magnate Ross Perot said, "In all my work with them, Ernie has been totally professional, totally constructive and a lot of fun to work with. They're the kind of people you need to accomplish things like major changes in the public schools."[11]

As the Texas IAF groups have gained in power and respect, most of the overt opposition to their activities has ceased or been relegated to right-wing Catholic groups in the Rio Grande Valley, which continued to picket Valley Interfaith meetings and harass Catholic Bishop John Fitzpatrick who maintained strong support for the organization. But most Texas commu nity leaders have generally heeded the warning of San Antonio's former mayor Henry Cisneros who advised Fort Worth and Austin business leaders to "play it cool" with the local Interfaith groups. Cisneros had been both an adversary and an ally of COPS, and he clearly preferred to be an ally. When the San Antonio mayor met with about 15 Austin business leaders shortly after Austin Interfaith was organized, he told them that he and San Antonio had learned to lived with COPS and respect Ernie Cortes. Austin's leaders could do it too, if they didn't overreact or panic. "Listen carefully to what the Interfaith groups say, rather than to how they say it," he advised.[12]

Pike Powers, the managing partner of the Austin office of the law firm of Fulbright & Jaworski, followed Cisneros' advice and invited Cortes to meet with Austin business leaders. "He handled himself marvelously and got almost unanimous acclaim as having made one of the best presentations they'd ever had," Powers said of Cortes. "It was a classic illustration of how some people want him to have horns and a tail, and after they got to see him they were not only pleasantly surprised, but also very impressed."[13]

The only notable exception to the developing trend of cooperation and conciliation with IAF organizations occurred in 1986 in Houston. TMO leaders had gathered 30,000 signatures to protest the Houston City Council's approval of a $159 million rate hike for Houston Lighting and Power, the privately owned utility company. While the petition drive was underway, HL&P, which had once come under bitter attack from COPS in San Antonio for the utility's cost overruns in building the South Texas Nuclear Project, circulated flyers to TMO-member churches denouncing the organization. The materials charged that TMO was a group whose "Chicago-based leadership misleads even its own well-intentioned members in exploiting causes to advance radical political aims."[14] Organizer Robert Rivera said that the utility officials also sent letters to business leaders in Dallas, Fort Worth, and Corpus Christi saying, in effect, "whatever you do, don't let these groups get off the ground because they can be dangerous." Houston's Catholic Bishop Fiorenza quickly put out a letter endorsing TMO's efforts to the same parishes that had received the HL&P flyers. The heavy-handed approach by HL&P made the utility the kind of political enemy the IAF loves to hate—one that pro-vides a motivation for further organizing, and TMO leaders felt that they came out on top in the exchange. But the HL&P tactics also reminded TMO—and Cortes—that the IAF organ-izations in Texas were still not universally accepted.

While never giving an inch when the legitimacy of the organ-izations was under attack, Cortes and his leaders have been somewhat more philosophical about "routine" political defeats. All of the IAF organizations, including the powerful COPS, have had their share of political defeats over the years. They have lost bond elections for neighborhood improvements or failed to win approval from city councils or school boards for specific projects. But Cortes has been sanguine about these losses—particularly in 1988 when COPS suffered a major bond election defeat in San Antonio. COPS' opposition failed to de-rail public financing for a city sports stadium—the Alamo-dome—supported by Mayor Cisneros and the business commu-nity. COPS preferred to spend public bond money on libraries, parks, or other neighborhood improvements. But the organi-zation was never able to get its message across—or its own members aroused—having to compete with a heavy television campaign, a unified business community, and the then-strong leadership of Mayor Cisneros.

"We were out-organized and out-spent," Cortes says. "But let's keep it in perspective. It's not life or death for us. It's just politics—it's all part of the process. Fortunately, we've moved beyond the point in Texas where one or two political losses dooms our entire effort."

Local losses, such as this, have obviously not affected the longevity of the IAF organizations or the growing strength of their operation at the statewide level. "The IAF groups have moved into the state arena," Bill Hobby said with some satis-faction. "They have kept the heat on, pushing for real reform. As many as 15 to 30 IAF leaders—Catholic nuns, homemakers, blacks, browns, working-class whites—have participated in strategy sessions with the governor or myself." And he added, "I am proud to have done my part in bringing Hispanic leaders such as Cortes . . . into the inner circle of Texas leadership."[15]

But being in the "inner circle" in Texas is not without its problems—particularly if you don't play by the "inner-circle rules." It is often more complicated to deal with the approval of politicians like Hobby than with the open hostility of a major corporation like Houston Lighting and Power. It is harder to hold friends to strict standards of political accountability than enemies. And it is hard to remind friends that they don't "own" you or control your agenda. Most community organizations are so grateful for the few crumbs thrown to them by "friendly" officials that they are fearful of jeopardizing the relationship—even when the official goes soft on issues or commitments that are important to them, or in extreme cases, demands actions that compromise the organization.

This is not the nature of the IAF relationship with Hobby, according to Cortes. He insists that Hobby gets no deferential treatment. In fact, the Hobby-Cortes relationship has had its share of strains. Hobby was particularly upset in 1986 when Valley Interfaith did not "save" three incumbent Rio Grande Valley legislators from going down to defeat in the Democratic primary election. Angry teachers, unhappy over some aspects of the public school reform legislation, had organized a massive campaign to defeat supporters of the education package. In the Valley, they were successful, and the defeat of several popular Hispanic legislators sent shudders all the way to Austin—which Hobby himself felt.

"The Interfaith network made a serious error in judgment by not helping those legislators," Hobby aide Tiede said. "It's still quid pro quo, no matter what they say."

What people don't understand is the distance the nonpartisan IAF organizations try to maintain from candidates and the traditional political party process, Cortes insists. The affected Valley legislators failed to take the teachers' threats seriously and did not wage serious reelection campaigns. "It was not up to us to do their work for them," Cortes asserts.

Cortes admits that there is a piece of him that wanted to "smooth" this over with Hobby and affected legislators. "But there is another piece of me that says—and really hopes—that politicians like Hobby know that we'll do what's right because it is what we think must be done and because it makes sense to us for the long term. We're not trying to become the king-makers or the new patróns of the 1990s who deliver votes on demand by some politician in Austin or Washington. Our goal is not to be liked by politicians. If we have to choose between like and respect, we choose respect. When we start worrying whether or not politicians like us . . . then we'll be just like everybody else."

15

We Are the Only Alternative

San Antonio, 1986

"Most people have come into our communities to destroy them . . . the Klan . . . the dope dealers . . . the developers. . . . The people have looked to their ministers to defend and protect them."[1]

The speaker is the Reverend Nehemiah Davis, the distinguished black pastor of the Mount Pisgah Baptist Church in Fort Worth. The setting is the modern new Catholic chancery of the archdiocese of San Antonio. The audience is a group of about 60 Catholic priests, Protestant ministers, and Texas community leaders from eight Texas Industrial Areas Foundation organizations who are meeting to get to know each other better and determine how they can exert statewide influence as a network. Some of them have driven 13 hours from El Paso to be at the meeting, and several of the El Paso representatives speak no English. So the low rumble of simultaneous translation from English to Spanish accompanies the dialogue, which is about power and how to solidify it locally and leverage it statewide.

The ministers and priests are also struggling with what Ernie Cortes describes as a strength of his network: its pluralism and diversity. What started out as a poor Catholic and Hispanic neighborhood political organization in San Antonio had expanded panded into a Texas network of organizations that now included blacks and Protestants, whites and the middle class.

At the Catholic chancery are representatives from three San Antonio IAF organizations: the Hispanic and Catholic COPS, the predominantly black East Side Alliance, and the Metropolitan Congregational Alliance, made up of middle-class Anglo North Siders who are about evenly divided between Catholics and Protestants. Houston is represented by The Metropolitan Organization, which had a growing base of black Protestant ministers, middle-class whites, and Hispanic Catholic parishes. Fort Worth in 1981 had developed a largely Protestant organization evenly divided between blacks and whites. The Fort Worth group called itself the Allied Communities of Tarrant County (ACT). Also present is Valley Interfaith, organized in 1983 and, with its 40 Catholic parishes, more like the Hispanic and Catholic COPS, which is also the case with the El Paso Interreligious Sponsoring Organization (EPISO). But the new Austin Interfaith is largely a Protestant organization, with strong representation from the capital city's black churches.

When all the leaders of these organizations come together for statewide meetings—which they do frequently—there is a mix of language, dialect, color, style, income, and education. The people are old and young, male and female, clergy and laity. The religious beliefs include Baptist fundamentalism, Lutheran certainty, Catholic mystery, Episcopalian order, Methodist activism, and Unitarian rationalism. Excitement is in the air at these meetings—even tension—and sometimes genuine confusion about how to work together.

Ernie Cortes feels the diversity most of all because he oversees almost 20 full-time paid organizers who run these organizations, training new political leaders and building surprisingly stable community institutions in the process.[2] Several of the IAF organizations had become regular players in their local decision-making structures. Almost all of them had achieved recognition for their ability to mobilize voters and influence key local elections. This recognition and the feeling that they had only scratched the surface of their potential led to a heightened sense of anticipation about the influence they might eventually wield in Texas politics. By the year 2000, Hispanics and blacks will constitute a majority of the Texas population less than 30 years old, with Hispanics alone representing almost 40 percent. Because of their strength among Texas Hispanics in San Antonio, the Rio Grande Valley, El Paso, and other places, and because of their potential strength in black urban communities, leaders of the Texas Interfaith Network, as they had begun to call themselves, feel that the future could be theirs.

But today at the Catholic chancery, the IAF leaders know that it will not be easy to build their statewide power. A thoughtful strategy will have to be devised.

To Nehemiah Davis, that meant focusing more time and attention on organizing Texas' black communities. He felt that if the IAF organizations wanted to expand their power, they had to bring more blacks into the network. Texas blacks represented 12 percent of the population, and black voters had the potential to expand their already significant voting blocks in Houston, Dallas, Fort Worth, and key areas of East Texas. For the network to be strong, Davis asserted, it had to reach out to those black communities, and the way to do that was to get more black ministers involved—not exactly an easy task.

"The black minister is a self-made man, a figure of autonomy and power," says Davis, who explains that although the preacher's power is limited in most cases, it is unique because it comes from the fusion of religion, politics, personality, and persecution that is peculiar to black experience. "We're suspicious and wary when organizers come around," Davis says. "We've had to fight hard to establish our bulwark of peace, and we're not willing to let just any intruder come in to tell us what we should be doing. When you come in, we're going to be real careful. We've got too much to lose."

The Reverend Davis is not speaking of his own suspicion; he is already a solid convert to the IAF-style of political organizing. In fact, he first invited IAF organizers to Fort Worth in 1981. Rather, today, he speaks of the barriers to IAF organizing, not only in his city but in black communities across the state. And Nehemiah Davis knows the reality of political barriers. In his 70s and long active in Forth Worth politics, Davis had ties to former U.S. House Speaker Jim Wright and a host of other politicians. Although that occasionally gave him access to power, it was not enough for him. As he aged, he discovered that he wanted more. He watched COPS' successes in San

Antonio, and he hungered for similar action in Fort Worth. He was drawn to the concepts of the Iron Rule and the one-on-one relationship building. He was willing to learn and change, despite a lifetime of successes in his own church and achievements in the civil rights movement. And change, he did.

"I am a better pastor because of all of this," he says. "I have better relationships. But it takes a long time to build this kind of organization. Many people lose spirit because they expect it to happen overnight. When it doesn't, they give up. Few people have that kind of persevering spirit that's built on vision."[3]

Ernie Cortes believes that Nehemiah Davis has both a persevering spirit and a vision for community that fits the kinds of political organizing the IAF is undertaking in Texas. So Cortes has taken the time to listen—and get others to listen—to Davis today.

"Davis is a great man, got great values," Cortes says. "He's been involved in politics so long that he's gotten everything he can from the current system. But he knows that the black community has to do something differently to get what it needs. He likes us, likes what we do, but he doesn't think we always understand."

So Davis had taken it on himself to educate Cortes and Catholic activists about the black community and to let them know that if they really wanted to develop new kinds of political leaders among working poor people in black communities, they would have to deal with black ministers first. That's because the IAF-style of institutional-based organizing cannot succeed without the most stable institution in black neighborhoods: the church—which often takes on the distinct personality of its pastor. IAF organizers had to understand the strong differences between the role of the parish church in a Hispanic neighborhood, with the authority of the priests and a supportive bishop, and the role of the church in the black community, with the autonomy and power of the ministers.

"That pastor has to be number one," Davis says.

Father Rosendo Urabazo, the urbane COPS leader who holds a doctorate in psychology and serves as pastor of the Immaculate Heart of Mary parish in San Antonio, nods his head in understanding. "It *is* different," he comments. "In the Catholic church, we priests are given a position, we're assigned a church. We can be as self-righteous and pompous as we like and as long as the bishop is happy, no one can touch us. But most black pastors have had to build their own organization, to claw their way up."

"Yes, yes," says the Reverend D.L. Ellison, a black Methodist minister, also from Fort Worth. "The black preacher bears a double burden. He catches hell from the folk and he catches hell from God, too. There's nothing between."

This kind of interplay between Catholic and Protestant clergy and layleaders has been fundamental to the success of the IAF organizations in Texas and elsewhere in the nation. The act of Protestant ministers "educating" Catholic priests within the walls of a Catholic chancery is typical of the behind-the-scenes ecumenicism that sustains the internal structure of the organizations. The effort to understand the practical as well as the spiritual aspects of their religious traditions has allowed IAF leaders to arrive at political decisions they can feel comfortable implementing. So when the Protestants and Catholics present a united front on certain community issues, it is hard for political leaders to ignore them. As such, the involvement of Protestants has become essential to the success of the broad-based community coalitions the IAF has established. Ironically, the Catholic bishops of Texas enabled the Texas IAF to reach out to Protestants in the first place.

The Texas Catholic Conference, the official organization of the 14 bishops of Texas, had carefully watched the develop-ment of San Antonio's COPS from the beginning. The bishops saw that COPS' victories were as beneficial to the Catholic church as to the neighborhoods on the West Side.

"After Vatican II, there was a move for Catholic pastors to share responsibility with laypeople in their congregations. But most pastors didn't know how to do it," according to Sister Maribeth Larkin. "Then COPS came along and showed them how."[4] As COPS developed local church leaders, these people naturally became more involved in the work of their parishes, and their efforts revitalized the churches as they did the neigh-borhoods. "Not one parish on the West Side of San Antonio died after COPS started," said Larkin, who served as an organ-izer for COPS after she left Los Angeles.

Thriving parishes in poor urban neighborhoods were a

matter of some interest to Texas Catholic bishops. And for a very simple, if not totally spiritual, reason: money. "If the neighborhood dies, the church dies," asserted former COPS president Andy Sarabia. "Then there's nobody to put money in the collection plate on Sunday."[5]

The late Father Dan Hennessey understood the issue of parish development very well. Pastor of St. James Church in southwest San Antonio, he was one of COPS' early vice presidents, and he once complained that he could only get about six pastors to come to COPS' first convention. "I told them, 'Guys, this is an insurance policy to keep our key leaders here in our parish.' They were all flying out to the North Side—the ones who could afford it—and taking a good chunk of our collection with them. Joining COPS is good economics. And it's good religion. I'm paying $3,000 a year to the chancery for insurance on these buildings; $1,500 [COPS' dues for his parish] is cheap to keep them from becoming a cemetery," Hennessey said.[6]

As strong as was the Catholic church's financial interest, it was not the only factor to motivate the bishops to support IAF organizing in San Antonio, Houston, and other areas later on. When Patrick Flores agreed to serve on COPS' initial sponsoring committee in 1973, the Vatican was grooming him to become the first Hispanic archbishop in the United States. A kindly, energetic man, Flores had served as auxiliary bishop to Archbishop Francis Furey in San Antonio and, for a brief time, as the bishop of El Paso. After Furey's death, Flores became archbishop in 1979, presiding over San Antonio's half million Catholics. Part of his mission, Flores felt, was to bring American Hispanics into the mainstream of both church and community. COPS' early successes had demonstrated to him that the organization could be a vehicle for both. In the early years of organizing, Flores had even sent letters to Catholic parish leaders urging them to attend COPS' meetings.[7] So it was Flores who helped set the stage for IAF organizing in Houston, Los Angeles, and El Paso, as well as in San Antonio. And it was to Flores that other Texas bishops began to look for guidance in how to deal with the IAF. Bishop Flores' positive guidance, plus the financial support of Catholic organizations, gave Ernie Cortes, Ed Chambers, and others the time to experiment with various techniques and training methods until they could develop the organizing formula that made them successful. The success attracted the Protestants, who brought new recruits, new energy, new money, and a new diversity to the effort. The diversity created a broader base for the organizations and allowed them to transcend single issues, self-righteousness, parochialism, and the rigidity that encompasses many community-based movements. And the "institutionalized" flexibility allowed the local IAF organizations to survive the perils and instability of grass-roots politics.

After more than 50 years of community organizing and several million dollars of Catholic and Protestant money, the IAF had finally hit on an approach that worked. COPS and Cortes had set the pattern that was being followed not only in Texas, but in New York, California, Maryland, Arizona, and other states. With the full-fledged establishment of the Texas network of organizations in 1983, the pattern became a harbinger of success.

Each of the fledgling organizations in Texas and elsewhere in the nation had both a financial and structural tie to the IAF. Financially, it came in the form of a contract in which each local organization paid for the training of its leadership, as well as for the consulting services of Ernie Cortes, Ed Chambers, and other IAF cabinet members. Cortes' and Chambers' salaries were paid by the IAF from the proceeds of such contracts. Structurally, the relationship centered on neighborhood churches, which formed the nucleus for all IAF organizing. Local interfaith coalitions of these churches would hire a professional organizer who had been trained by the IAF and who rotated among the various IAF-linked organizations every few years to keep personality cults from developing and to prevent local organizations from becoming totally dependent on any single organizer. The organizer, and perhaps a secretary, would be the only paid staff for the local organization. All other leadership roles would be filled by volunteers—the "natural leaders" in local church and community organizations. Although the organizers were hired and fired locally, with their salaries paid from locally raised funds, the organizers in Texas reported to Cortes. They also met frequently with Chambers and IAF organizers from other parts of the country. Because of the growing financial stability of the IAF and its local organizations, organizers could be paid a living wage—from about $24,000 to $50,000 annually depending on their experience and level of responsibility. This allowed the IAF to hold on to the expertise it had developed—something Alinsky had never been able to do. It also created an aura of "professionalism" among the IAF cadre of organizers, who developed an esprit de corps.

The organizer's main task was to recruit and train the volunteer leaders—and to teach. Organizers were expected to develop the same combination of inner strength and public skills as the people they trained, but they were also expected to learn how to develop a strategy to build the organization and to generate change in the community. Because the organizations had to be built around the values people would act on, organizers had to focus continually on the tension between the world as it is and the world "as it should be."[8] That meant organizers had to teach local leaders how to operate in the practical, hard-edged, cynical world of politics, while building a new world of justice and freedom. To do this, organizers had to have the maturity to understand the value of balance, moderation, and compromise. As such, the IAF did not recruit fresh-faced college kids. Instead, Cortes and Chambers looked for people with a wide range of experience in working with people and building other organizations. The men and women who became IAF organizers were usually veterans of other organizations— VISTA, the Peace Corps, social service agencies, labor unions, political clubs—and especially the church. About one-third of the IAF's permanent organizers were nuns, priests, ministers, or former associates of religious-oriented organizations.

Before an IAF organizer was hired, however, a local organization had to complete the first phase of development. Local people had to set up their own sponsoring committee, composed of representatives of churches or other religious-affiliated organizations such as charities, social service agencies, or religious orders. The sponsoring committee's job was to raise enough seed money to finance at least a two-year organizing effort, including money to pay a full-time organizer, cover office and clerical expenses, and contract with the IAF to set up leader training programs. In some cases, local sponsoring committees might enter into a "preorganizing" contract with the

IAF. These efforts occurred when a local committee needed help to raise the seed money—as did Fort Worth and Houston. In this situation, local ministers would put together an initial $10,000 or $15,000 to contract with the IAF to raise additional money and help put together a broad-based sponsoring committee. Only when the operating money was in the bank would an IAF organizer be interviewed and hired to begin the full-scale recruitment of leaders to run the new organization.

The sponsoring committee would assume the leadership for the organization for the first few years until there was a large enough membership base to become financially self-sufficient through dues payments from member churches—usually about 2 percent of a local church budget. At this point, a mass convention of members from all the affiliated churches would elect officers to direct the organization's future activities. The effort succeeded only if sponsors committed themselves to the process with both money and time. And each sponsoring committee in Texas quickly learned that success depended not on some hot-shot organizer from the national IAF; rather, it depended on what they did and how hard they were willing to work. They learned that powerful organizations could never be gifts from outside agitators. In the IAF system, a broad-based organization had to be built with local people and local money. When—and if—the effort succeeded, there would be no question about who owned the organization: it would belong to the people who built it. The Iron Rule was always the first rule to be learned on any IAF organizing project.

The central focus of both the organizing drive—and the maintenance of existing organizations—was a mixture of house meetings, one-on-one encounters, training sessions, "actions" in which members made presentations or demands to solve a specific local problem, and accountability sessions with public officials. The purpose of each of the activities was the development of skills and insights in leaders who understood power and who could operate effectively on behalf of their own self-interest and for the good of the community as a whole.

During the early days in Texas, Ed Chambers always assisted with fundraising for local sponsoring committees, often finding national church money from both Protestant and Catholic groups, particularly from the Catholic Campaign for Human

Development. Campaign staff then dispersed the money to community groups serving the poor. In Texas, every IAF organization received initial funding from the Campaign for Human Development, which had been founded by Monsignor John Egan, an old admirer of Saul Alinsky and board member of the IAF. The ties were so strong at one time between the IAF and the Catholic Campaign that former COPS president Beatrice Cortez became national chair of the campaign in 1985. Other COPS leaders such as Andy Sarabia were also policymakers within the Catholic organization.

The IAF itself developed a new governing structure that included Cortes as one of its five-member managing "cabinet." Chambers was the top-ranking member, along with other long-time IAF organizers Larry McNeil, Mike Gecan, and Arnie Graf. A noncontrolling national board provided financial and policy guidance in annual meetings.[9]

In addition to the United Neighborhoods Organization, three other Los Angeles-area organizations were established—the San Fernando Valley Organizing Committee, the East Valley Organization, and the South Central Organizing Committee. On the East Coast, organizations had been established in Queens, East Brooklyn, the Bronx, and Baltimore, with a host of sponsoring committee operations underway elsewhere. Phoenix had become the base for an expanding southwest strategy. Nationally, almost 50 full-time IAF organizers served about 1,000 affiliated churches. More than 3,500 ministers, priests, nuns, layleaders, and community activists had completed the IAF's intensive national training program. If all IAF local organizations were linked nationally, they would have a membership base of more than one million members. And the numbers, as well as IAF influence, were growing.

The single project that has brought an IAF organization the most acclaim—other than COPS—has been the Nehemiah Housing Project in Brooklyn. There, the IAF organization, East Brooklyn Churches, developed in the mid-1980s one of the most innovative efforts in the nation to provide home ownership to low-income families. Nehemiah was named for the biblical prophet who rebuilt the walls of ancient Jerusalem, and the *New York Times* called the project "a powerful example for community self-help."[10] In a joint venture with New York City, the IAF organization enabled almost 2,000 families to own their own homes, built on vacant land donated by the city, which also provided tax abatements for the improved property. Private builders constructed the single-family row houses and, in effect, created suburbs within inner-city neighborhoods. Construction financing came from an $8 million revolving fund put together by Ed Chambers and other IAF leaders with the financial support of Catholic, Episcopalian, and Lutheran church groups. The houses were sold at cost (about $45,000 in 1987), with New York City providing a form of mortgage subsidy. Roughly 40 percent of the first 1,000 buyers came from nearby public housing projects. People moved away from welfare and into middle-class home ownership.

While housing has been the target in Brooklyn, education issues have been the focus for other IAF organizations. Some groups have begun one-on-one organizing to build local public school–based groups. Although the primary purpose has been to increase parental involvement in local schools that serve low-income students, the IAF organizing strategy is to build new core constituencies among people who care about schools and education issues. In some communities, the IAF groups are taking the lead to set up city-wide business and school coalitions to provide guaranteed jobs or college scholarships for high school graduates who meet certain standards of achievement and attendance.

In 1988, the IAF groups joined nationally for the first time for a "Sign Up and Take Charge" campaign, pioneered in Baltimore. The purpose of the campaign was to build a national agenda of issues, growing out of the concerns of urban communities. Each local group selected issues for its area—housing, health care, drug abuse, education. Hundreds of thousands of signatures were collected—from non-IAF members. This kind of venture is part of the IAF process of experimentation. "We'll try it and if it works, we'll expand it," Cortes says.

Decisions about these kinds of projects and the direction of the IAF organizations are made by the IAF cabinet, whose members, like Cortes, serve as lead organizers and coordinators for individual organizations. The cabinet ultimately is accountable to the local organizations, which decide on the local or statewide projects they want to undertake. "They can pull the plug on us anytime they want to. They can disassociate. Our only source of funding is the contracts with the organizations," Cortes says.

Texas organizations have contracts with the IAF that total about $250,000, and by 1990, 20 trained IAF organizers served organizations in Texas, a heavier concentration than any other state. "We're stronger in Texas than elsewhere because we invested heavily there in the 1970s," Ed Chambers says. "We're just beginning to reach our critical mass there. People are beginning to see this—particularly the smart politicians, and they're getting nervous about it. They're not nice to our organizations because they like to be nice. They smell the future. We're the only alternative to people who want to participate in public life in a meaningful way. Otherwise you've got to play the electoral politics game, which takes a lot of money, a good pollster, and someone to craft you for television. It's a sham. You can't call that democracy."

16

There Is No Substitute
for the Fire

Austin, 1986

Ernie Cortes and I join Ernie's wife Oralia and several of his
Texas organizers in the bar of the Ramada Inn on the south
bank of the Colorado River. The hotel is old, rather shabby,
and off the beaten track for the legislators and lobbyists who
flock into Austin for politics and business. So it is quiet this
Friday evening. We can talk and relax. Robert Rivera, who has
just become a new father, is there, along with two Catholic
sisters—Pearl Ceasar and Mignonne Konecny—who are organizing in El Paso and Fort Worth. The group is awaiting the
arrival of Sister Christine Stephens and other organizers from
around the state who are coming to Austin for a meeting of
organizers from each of the local organizations. Cortes brings
them together frequently, and their meetings are both joyful
reunions and serious strategy sessions. And there are reports—
progress reports, book reports, research reports—even "scout-
ing" reports for new people and new ventures. Cortes usually
presides and often tells the organizers, "I'll give you three minutes to talk if you're good, but if you're boring I'll cut you off
in 30 seconds." So the meetings are punchy, packed with information, and laced with good humor. A meeting is scheduled for
the next day. Tonight, the organizers are just glad to see one

another, reflecting a comfortable camaraderie that has built up among them over the years.

Most of the Texas organizers served an apprenticeship with COPS in San Antonio where they developed their vision of what a community organization should be. Part of their training was to hold as many as 10 one-on-one meetings a day—meetings with community people, business leaders, government officials, or church leaders. Then, they were to reflect on what they heard.

"In COPS the organizers didn't have to make many phone calls to get a turnout for an action. People did it for themselves," Robert Rivera says.[1]

"Yeah . . . we taught them the right way in San Antonio," Cortes jokes.

"Well, they were raised with action in COPS," Rivera retorts. "That was the culture in COPS. It's harder to build that into the other organizations, but we try."

The way to develop the culture, Cortes explains, is to get a taste for victory. "COPS had a taste for victory from the beginning," he says. "When we went into Houston and El Paso, before we had a chance for victory, the other side nearly killed us. In San Antonio, we had a jump on them, a year or so of quiet organizing. In El Paso, they went after us after we'd been organizing only six months."

Without having the time to learn and reflect, to act and evaluate, leaders cannot develop the self-confidence to withstand strong challenges, much less virulent attacks. Cortes explains that the early, quiet, behind-the-scenes organizing and training is critical for the success of the organizations. Also, the first public action has to be planned with the possibility of success within reach. People have to know what it feels like to win something they want. In El Paso, the Industrial Areas Foundation almost failed because the attacks by right-wing Catholics forced the El Paso Interreligious Sponsoring Organization's leaders to go public before they were ready. They were so busy defending themselves that they had little opportunity to initiate an action they might win.

But the El Paso organization eventually did win, and by 1983, the IAF had organizations in Houston, San Antonio, Fort

Worth, the Rio Grande Valley, and Austin. By 1990, the groups had a statewide reputation, local church affiliations with a membership base of at least 400,000, several hundred well-trained leaders, and a developing relationship with officeholders and business leaders who held power in Texas. New organizations were coming along in Fort Bend County, outside of Houston, and in the Winter Garden area of the Texas border between Laredo and Del Rio. Talks were underway for sponsoring committees in Corpus Christi and other cities. You could follow the progress of these local organizations through their own press clippings, just as I had once traced the growth of COPS in the cold little office in the old school at Immaculate Heart of Mary.

The new organizations were also moving beyond the stereotypes of traditional poor people's organizations. They accepted no government money. They did not manage employment or loan programs. They did not endorse candidates. Their members did not turn up on the payrolls of powerful politicians. And still they thrived.[2] They came back year after year with new issues, new ideas, and new leaders with the same firm resolve: to hold politicians—and each other—accountable to the needs of the wider community and the common good.

Cortes believes it is the quality of leaders developed in the organizations that makes it all possible. "You can't have people who are just against things," he says. "You have to be *for* things. During the first years of COPS, I selected a leader who was an unguided missile. She was good in action, she liked conflict. But she'd fight everybody . . . the politicians, me, the other leaders. She turned out to be a disaster. Because relationships are important to us, you can't operate with people like this. We invite them out. You have to find people who have a sense of humor, who like people, who like their families, and who are more balanced. They are the kinds of people you can build with."

For Cortes, the building of relationships outlives the demands of the immediate issue. And, if there is one concept that he preaches as much as the Iron Rule, it is that there are "no permanent enemies." "You don't vanquish or obliterate your foes," he says. "You leave them enough dignity to fight another day. When power is won, it has to be used judiciously. It has to be accountable and used in accordance with the values of fair play and respect for the individual."

Even after some of his organizations' most heated confrontations, Cortes taught his leaders to start a "healing" process to repair any damage to political or personal relationships. He recounts how one-time foe San Antonio banker Tom Frost now works with COPS on projects of mutual interest and even contributes money to some of COPS' special efforts. Frost's bank lobby had been where COPS members changed pennies into dollars and back again while Cortes was upstairs with Frost telling the banker that his words were just "balderdash."

Now, years later, Cortes tells of another meeting with Frost. "We're [meeting] with Mr. Frost and a couple of other very powerful business people about the South Texas Nuclear Power Project, and we're saying we think there ought to be some accountability in cost controls and they're saying 'we couldn't be more in agreement with you. . . .' After the meeting is over, Mr. Frost walks up to me and says, 'Balderdash, wasn't it!' Now he tells everybody what good friends we are. . . . Different time, different place, different situation, different issue. No permanent enemies, no permanent friends. Just interests, permanent interests."[3]

Cortes is proud that most IAF leaders and organizers understand and practice this approach. "I think I understood the power of relationships in a personal sense," says Christine Stephens, who has joined our group. "You learn that in a family. You know you can't exist by yourself. But I never carried over what I knew into a political setting. In that sense, I was politically illiterate when I got into this."

Cortes explains that just as survival in a family depends on relationships, so does survival in politics—especially the IAF kind of politics that relies on a sense of community and responsibility within each local organization. "But we are not a substitute family," Cortes says. "While we can never do for each other in our organizations what a family ought to do for its members, we can teach each other how to develop trust in a relationship with people who are not part of our families. That trust comes from learning to be honest and accountable to each other."

When IAF members move outside of their organizations to

develop relationships with politicians and others who hold power, there is an added dimension. "We want to learn from political leaders," Cortes says. "But we also expect them to learn from us. It works both ways. It is a process of arguing, bargaining, trading, and negotiating, and we expect to participate in it. Only then can some form of public trust emerge."

For IAF leaders, this means learning the difference between always having to be right on every issue and understanding the need to compromise now and then. And compromise requires some flexibility—not always easy for people who bring moral values to politics.

"I've always been a person for whom principle has been important," Stephens says. "I really had to learn the importance of being 'unprincipled' in terms of developing relationships."[4] For Stephens, this meant learning to withhold judgment and avoid stereotyping people just because she happened to disagree on a specific issue. It also meant learning to be "reasonable."

"Getting your way all the time may be right," Cortes taught her. "But it may not be reasonable because the other person might lose everything. You have to take into consideration that it is important for others not to lose everything."

Cortes taught his organizers that it was okay to polarize in the arena of action because they needed to do something dramatic to get recognition. But organizers had to remember, he constantly reminded, that things are not always black and white. "In an action, you act as if the enemy is 100 percent wrong, but you know that he may only be 60 percent wrong, and this is why you leave him some dignity," Cortes says. "You have to have some humor about it. You have to exercise some restraints. That's what politics is—restraints, boundaries, things you won't do because it's not war, it's only politics. All's fair in love and war. But this is not about war. We're talking about politics. Ultimately, it's about making a deal both sides can live with. It's not just electoral activity."

With this approach, politics could become more than a periodic contest between "good guys and bad guys." Issues would change. Positions would shift. Coalitions could be developed or dissolved. But solid human relationships would remain.

In national training programs, Ed Chambers repeatedly

taught IAF leaders that "people without power cloak themselves in statements of principle. They have all of this rhetoric
about insulted honor, and they deal in righteous indignation.
They think they have the favor of God. But that's all movement
talk . . . not the language of people who really understand and
hold power. It's neither fresh nor thoughtful."

Ed Chambers and Ernie Cortes believe they are training the
new political leaders of the 1990s—and that they have hit an
effective method to do it that is both fresh and thoughtful. "Tip
O'Neill says it," Chambers reminds. "All politics is local politics.
Damn right! But where are the local organizations? We've got a
few—and there's no local competition for us. As a result, our
people are going to be on the city councils, planning commissions . . . they'll be the new generation of blacks and Hispanics
that are going to be running things in our cities."

If Chambers is correct, and if the IAF organizations continue
to expand in Texas, the Southwest, California, New York, and
along the eastern seaboard, a new generation of working-class
citizens could begin to affect American politics in the 1990s.
And if Texas is the model, these new leaders will be pulled
from the middle of the political spectrum—from people who
value family, church, and community. They will be people who
have not succumbed to the political right, which has let ideology
overtake reason and common sense, nor to the political left,
which has let its sacred cows inhibit clear thinking and decisive
action. They will be the people for whom Democratic or Republican party ties and partisan rituals, such as they remain, are
empty. They will be people not easily co-opted or misled by
politicians, the media, or business and labor leaders. They will
be people who question and probe the economic and political
policies that shape their communities, just as they question and
probe the personal experiences that shape their individual lives
and families. They will be the people—like the thousands who
initiated significant political action in COPS and the newer IAF
organizations—whose anger is justified and fired by action and
who use its energy to generate victory for their neighbors and
community.

To continue finding these people, these new political leaders
of the 1990s, Ernesto Cortes still searches for something basic

within each of them: anger. The search springs from his belief that change can occur when people connect their personal anger with an awakening compassion for others, and then, in turn, transform that anger into constructive political action. Anger, for Cortes, equals energy, and energy is necessary for action to help yourself and your neighbors.

When COPS held its first election of officers in 1973, Cortes insisted that candidates have two main qualifications: concern for people and anger. But Cortes was not looking for mere verbal violence, the kind that spurts forth on a dragon's tongue and destroys whatever is within its reach. Instead, he wanted in his leaders the kind of anger that probes for truth and challenges the injustices of life. He realized the kind of abiding anger he was looking for arises most often from some deep personal experience, from the feelings aroused by absorbing injuries, injustices, or wrongs that burn like an unquenchable fire within. Cortes has undertaken the formidable task of helping people come to terms with their anger and turn it into a useful political tool.

To make his point, he often tells of the experiences of an EPISO leader. The middle-class, middle-aged woman, visited an elementary school in Socorro, a community of about 20,000 people outside of El Paso where 3,000 families lived without running water. The area was once incorporated, but long ago disbanded any form of government and existed in a kind of bureaucratic limbo as long as the city of El Paso refused to extend water lines or any other form of public services. Sewage was disposed of through septic tanks that overflowed when it rained, allowing waste to seep into the soil. This waste would find its way into the underground water supply, which was brought back to the surface in the wells some Socorro residents had to use for cooking and bathing. The EPISO leader, a volunteer tutor, spent some time in a Socorro classroom with a pretty little girl about 7 years old who had a horrendous odor. It took several weeks before the volunteer realized that the odor existed not because the child was dirty, but because in an effort to become clean and fresh like some of her classmates, the little girl was bathing regularly in the contaminated well water. This awareness made the woman feel physically sick, a feeling that stayed with her for months. She had always loved to take bubble baths, but she could no longer enjoy that small indulgence.

"For six months, I couldn't take a bath in a tub full of water. I would ration out only a small amount," the woman told Cortes. Then she realized that her own bizarre behavior occurred because she was brooding about the Socorro child and the damage the contaminated water was doing to her body and mind. The more she thought about it, the angrier she became, particularly with herself because she couldn't push images of the child from her mind. She was so disturbed that one Sunday after Mass she cornered her parish priest and told him about it. The priest listened calmly and said that denying herself a bath and worrying about it didn't help anyone. "If you're angry about the little girl," the priest said, "do something to help the people of Socorro get water!"

The priest's challenge and her haunting memory of the malodorous child led to an effort on the part of EPISO to bring water to Socorro, an effort that eventually succeeded.

Cortes believes that this kind of memory of a personal experience, especially when it arouses anger, has a power and force of its own. "Anger is something very deep and it is rooted in memory," he says. "It's not just a spur-of-the-moment kind of thing. It is tied to loss, grief, and it is rooted in relationships and concerns with other people."

Because Cortes, the organizer and teacher, is also a storyteller, he reaches back into his most fertile source of stories—the Old Testament—and recounts a tale of Moses. "Moses was raised as a prince of the House of Egypt. He had all the good things of life, but he identified with the outsiders. He was one of them. He killed an Egyptian overseer who was abusing a Hebrew. He was angry because the Hebrew he helped told others. Moses was frightened and ran away, but he couldn't forget the people he left behind. The memory of their oppression is so strong it is like a burning bush, a fire that never goes out, an unquenchable fire. That memory is powerful, has a force of its own. It's hallowed ground. That's what we mean by anger," he says.

Most people feel uneasy with the prospect of using their anger, so they suppress it or deny it, only to have it appear hot and uncontrollable at inappropriate times and places. Cortes works with the leaders he develops to get them to remember their personal anger, to understand its sources, and then to draw on it as fuel for the energy they need to confront those who hold power over their lives. "I'm talking about the ability to get angry and act at an appropriate time and place," Cortes explains. "Anger has to be related to the classical virtue of prudence. It has to be controlled and connected to a concern for someone else—like when a parent is angry with a child; there has to be a restraint to the action connected with anger."

Again and again, people within the IAF organizations returned to their feelings of anger. Many were like Sister Christine Stephens, who had systematically smothered her anger and felt an overwhelming psychological release when she could confront it legitimately. "First you learn not to be afraid of it and to understand that others are not necessarily afraid of it either. It was wonderful to learn that there are people in this world for whom anger is not a terrifying experience," she said.

The kind of deep, burning anger that Stephens and others in Cortes' network talk about comes from something seething inside of them, something they were deprived of, an event or a pattern of experiences that is fundamentally unfair, which helped mold their beliefs and, more importantly, endowed them with a sense of empathy for people similarly hurt. It is the kind of anger that is connected to a passion for people, and it never develops into revenge because there are other values to hold it in control.

"In the world out there, it's dog eat dog, go for the gold enchilada," said Rudy Enriquez, who spent 25 years working for a meat-packing plant in San Antonio. Many of his friends were hurt on the job or were laid off over the years, and his bitterness grew as he thought about the absent owners of the plant who did not know or care about the people whose lives were ruined by their experiences there. "It seems to me that some people enjoy seeing other people down. If I wasn't a Christian, I think I could make a list and I would blow some brains out, not for myself, but for people I've known who cannot defend themselves."[5]

Enriquez was attracted to COPS because a friend told him the organization provided a way to use that anger, to control it in a positive way in the political arena to help himself and his neighbors. But Enriquez found more than that. He believes that COPS has helped people keep their anger from eroding their souls into shells of selfishness and bitterness. "Over the years, I've seen people . . . mellow. In the early years, it was 'hey, I want my street fixed first!' Now people wait for communities that need it more," he said.[6]

Enriquez, along with hundreds of others, learned that successful political action cannot be based on hot anger or impulse. But they have recognized its role in their motivation for action.

Cortes believes that people like Enriquez—who are willing to grow, change, mellow, and understand how to use their anger—are essential to the institutionally based organizing he has been engaged in since the early 1970s. "We're not going to build the kind of power organizations that we're talking about unless we find a few good people who understand power, who are committed to other people, who are willing to act on their anger, who see their anger as a tool, to be willing to adjust it or willing to synthesize it with humor and perspective," he says.[7]

And Ed Chambers agrees. "There is no substitute for the fire," he says. "You have to have a vision that you're on the side of the underdog, the have-nots. You've got to use your wits, your talents, your brain, your imagination, your energy to go for the underdog. All our best leaders have that anger. It doesn't hurt if it's hot originally. If it's hot, you can turn it down to cold. But if it's not there . . . you've got nothing to work with."

Epilogue

Austin, 1990

Ernesto Cortes values politics. So do I. It is one of the magnets that drew me through life, as well as to the pursuit of this story. But Cortes has moved the practice of politics to a plane higher than that on which our most experienced and powerful politicians play out their roles. Cortes understands the view of British political writer Bernard Crick who believes that "politics . . . is the activity by which differing interests . . . are conciliated by giving them a share in power in proportion to their importance to the welfare and survival of the whole community."[1]

The key words here are "conciliation" and "share." They represent fundamentally different concepts from more strident words such as "usurp" or "control." Ernesto Cortes understands that working poor people in the United States rarely have total control of anything, and it is unlikely that they can usurp power. The reality of the American political system at the end of the 20th century is that power follows money. And political power most often derives from economic power. Only the most blatant abuses of economic power create a demand from people for political moves to restrict or regulate it, and then, only temporarily. But "organized" middle-class and working poor people, if they are informed and willing to take responsibility for the kind of "internal revolution" the Industrial

Areas Foundation promotes, might be able to provide some balance to "organized" money. They might be able to prevent themselves from being its victims. They might even acquire a large enough share of political power to shape not only their own lives, but the welfare of the common community.

For IAF leaders, the process of getting a share of power involves teaching, nurturing, confronting, negotiating, compromising, giving, receiving. It also involves settling for only part of what they want, because if they hold out for everything, they most likely will get nothing. And the IAF leaders I met would always take something rather than nothing.

I guess this is one of the facets of IAF organizing that so attracted me when I began this political voyage several years ago. Cortes, Ed Chambers, Sister Christine Stephens, Andy Sarabia, Nehemiah Davis, Robert Rivera, and the other articulate leaders I encountered held out a vision of the "world as it should be," but they operated in the "world as it is." Which meant that they understood political reality. More importantly, they usually seemed to know the difference between reality and political fantasy, something even seasoned politicians get confused. They learned the difference between being right and being effective, and they learned that choosing to be effective could sometimes be the wiser choice. They learned that they had to be tough to achieve what many of the church people called "goodness." They learned that in some circles, their toughness gave a bad name to their goodness. But they also learned that toughness and goodness could be a winning combination, especially when they operated from the strength of numbers, the power of knowledge, the clarity of goals, and the courage of convictions.

I was also drawn to Cortes and his leaders because they saw power as more "relational" than coercive. For them, power had a dimension of being "acted upon" as well as acting, of being influenced, as well as influencing. They viewed power almost as a reciprocal "relationship." In fact, the concept of relationship was central to everything—leadership, power, organizing, learning. I, too, had learned the value of relationships. But I had never been able to articulate it, much less use it as an operating principle of political behavior or motivation.

Cortes valued the kinds of relationships that grow out of association with neighbors, co-workers, church members, school associates, people with whom you share action. The IAF organizations even valued relationships with adversaries, leaving the door open for adversaries to become allies in future causes. So for Cortes, working within the political system meant working with the people who ran the system—a far cry from the political jujitsu tactics of Saul Alinsky. But even more importantly, Cortes, Ed Chambers, and other IAF leaders understood how to develop and sustain relationships *within* their organizations—relationships built not only on affinity, but on accountability. This internal responsibility to each other and the group allowed the IAF organizations to survive while other grass-roots movements faded away. At this writing, COPS—the model—is almost 20 years old and still is a major factor in San Antonio politics.

Cortes, Chambers, and the other IAF leaders have learned what Tocqueville saw in the American experiment: that group loyalties are an important intermediary between society and the state.[2] Totalitarian regimes always destroy intermediary groups so that nothing stands between the government and the individual. The individual is isolated and has no protection, no shield, no privacy, no advocate. But the precarious nature of our market-driven economy and the mass entertainment/mass consumer orientation of our culture can produce an isolation that is almost as debilitating and deadly for the soul as any oppressive regime. So there is a void in American politics between people and their government, between the governed and the governing, between the powerless and the powerful. The danger, as Ed Chambers points out, is real. "If families and churches don't develop 'institutional power,' they will be dominated by the huge corporations, the mass media and the experts in our 'benevolent' government," he wrote.[3]

Yet where they exist, the IAF city-based interfaith groups have managed to fill the void. The IAF groups have provided the associations, the friendships, the shared experiences, the protections, the training, the supports, and the shields that make true citizenship possible. They have developed both an individual and a group confidence, both a personal and political empowerment. This is one reason I believe the groups are effective and long-lasting. They provide a profound sense of "belonging" and an equally strong sense of "transcending."

The Viennese psychiatrist Viktor Frankl, a World War II concentration camp survivor, made an intensive study of meaning. He says there is no one meaning in life, but many meanings, and that all meanings grow out of transcending a narrow sense of self. For Frankl, that can happen in three ways: by creating a work or significant deed, by encountering or experiencing something or someone that captures your attention and imagination, and by growing and developing in spite of the process of suffering.[4] It seems to me that the IAF organizations provide a way for large numbers of individuals to find meaning: The local IAF organizations have compiled records of significant deeds; they have enabled people to encounter other individuals and situations that stimulate their imagination and generate significant relationships; and they have provided a mechanism to allow people to grow and develop in spite of past or present economic or social deprivation. They have allowed people to transcend themselves and become a part of a larger community.

Within the IAF organizations has arisen a network of friends—the essence of community. And members of this community seem to enjoy one another's company, are useful to one another, and have established a powerful bond to one another because they share a common commitment to something larger than self. The result is that they begin to control their destiny—in cooperation with others. People who do this are not poor, no matter what their economic condition. They are strong. In Texas, these strong people are shaping a new grass-roots politics. They are changing their cities. They are influencing public policy in their state. They are capturing a "share" of power—of life and meaning. Once they have these experiences, no other politics seems as rich, satisfying, or productive.

By telling their stories to each other again and again, these people are also creating traditions among the working poor in certain neighborhoods across Texas and the nation. The stories of the department store and bank tie-ups, the housewives who corner the city manager, the old men buried with their COPS buttons, the politicians who beg for forgiveness, the negotiations to bring water to the *colonias,* the battles to put sewers in San Antonio's West Side, the petition drives that get the attention of big city mayors—all of these are told and retold. As such, they develop the force of legends, and legends have the ability to inspire and inform—even empower.

If politics is a marketplace[5]—the price mechanism of all social demands—then what the IAF groups have done is to enter the competition and maybe even change it. The IAF organizations may also lift the quality of the other entrants into the marketplace, perhaps even drive out the politicians and local bosses who consistently produce a public policy of shoddy goods. They may even inject a much-needed new vitality into the political market, which is overrun by deadening manipulation by experts and professionals who have taken over the process.

The novelist Ward Just once wrote a story that posed the question, "what do men want from politics?" He gave the answer in his title: *Honor, Power, Riches, Fame and the Love of Women.* Well, maybe. The idea, which is the same for women as well as men, is that people are in politics for only the obvious satisfactions. Perhaps some people do find honor, power, riches, fame, and love within the community-based IAF organizations, but that is not what the IAF culture promotes. And although it may be difficult for sophisticated observers to believe the organizations actually discourage this, the motivations of IAF organizers and leaders seem to me to have a depth of feeling that forces them to seek more than the obvious rewards of playing the political games.

When I described the political "culture" within the IAF organizations to the aide to a prominent Texas officeholder, he was skeptical. "Are these people for real?" he asked. Like the aide, we *should* be skeptical when we encounter something extraordinary or out of the range of our experience or even something that appears "too good to be true." We should look for any holes and hypocrisy. Yet, the IAF organizations at their best *are* operating outside of the range of our recent political experience. They are not playing at being political brokers or losing their sense of purpose in the horse race atmosphere of electoral politics. They seem to be developing systems of accountability and incorporating their religious values into a grass-roots democracy. They seem to be practicing a politics of joy and inclusion. They seem to be motivated by a concern for the common good. And they seem to expand our view of what that common good might be.

After several years observing their activities, I came to believe in them. Yet I still recognize how hard it is for sophisticated political veterans to take at face value someone like COPS leader Father Rosendo Urabazo when he says, "We need to look into our neighborhoods and see who is poor and needy. We have to . . . stand with those people who need us most."[6]

Or Ed Chambers when he says, "I feel distraught about the treatment of poor people. I want to correct that."

Or Sister Christine Stephens, who says that what is important is the "process" of becoming a true community.

Or Sister Maribeth Larkin when she says, "The important thing is how we grow and how we're doing."

Or even Ernesto Cortes when he says that people within the IAF organizations "recognize the importance of a search for values, a search for meaning, a search for an approach to public life which is more about understanding life and meaning than just dealing with a particular issue."

Cortes admits that skepticism is important, but he feels that it is inappropriate to apply it only to the poor—and not to the powerful. "There is a value called justice," he believes. "There are things that should not be taken from people. There should be a place where all are equal, where all can come with dignity. In the Old Testament, that place was the court at the gates of every city. Anyone could speak there. What we're about now is speaking and acting at the gates of the city. We want to develop a framework, a public philosophy which is suitable for the turn of the century, which speaks to people who have families, who care about communities, who have values, who care about work. We want to build up a tradition which goes to the roots of where people are, but which at the same time enables them to act in a public way. The political parties are in disarray. The movements have faded away . . . so we feel we have to do it on our own."

Something happened to me when I listened to Ernesto Cortes speak like this. It also happened when I interviewed dozens of people in the IAF organizations, sat in on hundreds of hours of meetings, read the old news clips, and watched the list of accomplishments grow.

I came to this story with a political experience shaped by skepticism. But I leave the story with an experience shaped by hope. Perhaps it is possible, after all, for men and women from all walks of life to continue the process of becoming "we, the people," and to grow fully into themselves as human beings by transcending themselves in the cause of both serving and teaching "the least of these." Perhaps there is still a place at the gates of the city—the entrance to our marketplace of politics—where all people can enter and act with dignity.

Chapter Notes

Chapter One

1. Ernesto Cortes, Jr. addressed 200 farmers and farm activists from 40 states as part of a Farm Crisis Workers Conference in Dallas, 20 July 1986. The conference was sponsored by the Texas Department of Agriculture and Farm Aid. The *Texas Observer* made a tape recording of Cortes' remarks and published excerpts in its 11 July 1986 issue in an article by Cortes titled "Organizing the Community." This account is derived from the unedited transcript of the tape, most of which did not appear in the *Observer*. I have seen Cortes present the material in several other workshop settings.

2. "The *Esquire* Register, 1988," *Esquire,* December 1988, 93.

3. Tim Richardson, "20 Who Hold the Power in Texas," *Texas Business Magazine,* February 1986, 59.

4. Cortes paraphrased a passage from Numbers 11:4–6: "Now the rabble that was among them had a strong craving; and the people of Israel also wept again, and said, 'O that we had meat to eat! We remember the fish we ate in Egypt for nothing, the cucumbers, the melons, the leeks, the onions and the garlic; but now our strength is dried up, and there is nothing at all but this manna to look at.'"

5. Numbers 11:16–17.

Chapter Two

1. State Treasurer Ann Richards toured the Rio Grande Valley *colonias* at the invitation of Valley Interfaith, 1 February 1988. Richards won the Democratic party nomination for governor in 1990.

2. Turner Collie Braden Inc. for the Texas Water Development Board, "A Reconnaissance Level Study of Water Supply and Wastewater Disposal Needs of the Colonias of the Lower Rio Grande Valley," January 1987.

Chapter Three

1. Because the Texas constitution prohibits debt financing, the legislature has to seek voter approval of a constitutional amendment any time it wants to issue bonds for capital improvements—prisons, water projects, public buildings, etc. Bonds for water improvements in the *colonias* were approved by Texas voters in a constitutional amendment election November 1989.

2. In 1988, Texas Agriculture Commissioner Jim Hightower was able to arrange a grant from private sources that provided a water hookup from the road to the homes of residents in the *colonia* of La Meza.

3. Dave Denison, "An Agenda for Progress," *Texas Observer*, 10 February 1989, 6.

4. Ernesto Cortes, Jr., training session for Texas Interfaith Network leaders, San Antonio, 15 February 1986.

5. Harry Boyte, *Community Is Possible* (New York: Harper & Row, 1984), 128.

6. Henry Cisneros served as mayor of San Antonio from 1981 to 1989. Still enormously popular, he chose not to run for reelection while in the midst of family difficulties. COPS and Cisneros had a close and complex relationship during his tenure as mayor, alternately assisting and attacking each other.

7. This exchange was recounted by the wife of a Mondale adviser who overheard the remark on the airport tarmac in Harlingen, Texas.

8. Metropolitan Congregational Alliance meeting, 2 December 1985, San Antonio.

9. Jan Jarboe, "COPS Eighth Anniversary, A Pep Rally for the People," *San Antonio Express*, 15 November 1981, n. pag.

Chapter Four

1. The Metropolitan Congregational Alliance and the East Side Alliance, both IAF organizations in San Antonio, merged in 1989 to form The Metro Alliance.

2. Author's interview with Mary Moreno, 22 February 1986, San Antonio.

3. Mary Moreno dropped out of IAF activities in late 1988 because she wanted to begin taking courses to get a college degree in education. Moreno said, "I may leave MCA, but MCA will never leave me. I learned skills for life there, and I apply what I learned everyday." In 1990, Moreno spent her free time trying to get the Catholic archdiocese of San Antonio to establish more Spanish-language services.

Chapter Five

1. Author's interview with Sister Maribeth Larkin, 12 February 1986, San Antonio.

2. Bishop Charles Grahmin was named bishop of the Catholic diocese of Dallas in 1990.

3. Unless otherwise noted, all Cortes quotations are taken from a series of interviews and conversations with the author from 1985 to 1989.

4. Geoffrey Rips, "In Which the Present Editor Bids an Affectionate Adios," *Texas Observer,* 9 January 1987, n. pag.

5. From "Historical Essays, and Studies, Appendix," letter to Bishop Mandell Creighton, in *Dictionary of Quotations,* ed. Robert Hyman (Lincolnwood, Illinois: National Textbook Company, 1985), 9.

6. Hans Kung, *On Being A Christian* (Garden City: Image Books, Doubleday & Company, 1984), 487.

7. Saul Alinsky, *Rules for Radicals* (New York: Random House, 1971), 51.

8. Author's interview with Edward T. Chambers, 10 July 1986, Los Angeles. Unless otherwise noted, all subsequent quotations from Chambers are taken from the same interview.

Chapter Six

1. The Industrial Areas Foundation holds three national training programs each year, rotating the site. This session took place at Mount St. Mary's College, Los Angeles, 8–18 July 1986. All quotations in this chapter are from workshops the author attended.

Chapter Seven

1. Democratic Governor Mark White was defeated in November 1986 by former Republican Governor William P. Clements, whom White had turned out of office in 1982. White tried to come back in 1990 but was defeated in the Democratic primary.

2. Author's interview with Sister Christine Stephens, 21 May 1986, Austin. Unless otherwise noted, all subsequent quotations from Stephens are taken from the same interview.

3. Author's interview with Mary Moreno, 22 February 1986, San Antonio.

Chapter Eight

1. These actual words appeared in a newspaper advertisement for County Commissioner Ollie Wurzbach, *San Antonio News,* 6 May 1966. The same sentiment was conveyed in similar words in the "black hand" television spot.

2. Calvin Trillin, "U.S. Journal: San Antonio," *The New Yorker,* 2 May 1977, n. pag.

3. John A Booth and David R. Johnson, "Power and Progress in San Antonio Politics, 1836–1970," in *The Politics of San Antonio,* ed. David R. Johnson, John A. Booth, and Richard J. Harris (Lincoln: University of Nebraska Press, 1983), 3–27.

4. Colleen O'Connor, "High Profile: Ernesto Cortes," *Dallas Morning News,* 3 January 1988, Section E, 1-3.

5. Quoted by Jan Jarboe, "Who Pulls the Strings in San Antonio?" *The Magazine of San Antonio,* undated clipping in the files of Communities Organized for Public Service, San Antonio.

6. Robert Brischetto, Charles L. Cotrell, and R. Michael Stevens, "Conflict and Change in the Political Culture of San Antonio in the 1970s," in *The Politics of San Antonio,* 76.

7. The Mexican American Unity Council today is a multiservice center that includes mental health and family services, business and economic development, as well as a neighborhood housing service program. Its funding comes from both private and public sources.

Chapter Nine

1. Recounted by Alinsky in *Rules for Radicals*, 141–43.

2. P. David Finks, *The Radical Vision of Saul Alinsky* (New York: Paulist Press, 1984), xi.

3. Ibid., 26.

4. Ibid., 148.

5. Boyte, *Community Is Possible*, 127.

6. Finks, *The Radical Vision*, 24.

7. Saul D. Alinsky, *Reveille for Radicals* (New York: Vintage Books, 1969), 6.

8. Alinsky, *Rules for Radicals*, 23.

9. For a discussion of these influences on Alinsky, see Joan E. Lancourt, *Confront or Concede, The Alinsky Citizen-Action Organization* (Lexington, Massachusetts: D.C. Heath and Company, 1979).

10. Alinsky, *Rules for Radicals*, 18.

11. Finks, *The Radical Vision*, 75.

12. Ibid., 167.

13. Ibid., 259.

14. Boyte, *Community Is Possible*, 133.

15. Alinsky, *Rules for Radicals*, 21.

16. Ibid., 127.

17. Ibid., 130, 128, 127, 128, 129.

18. FIGHT, the IAF organization in Rochester, was an acronym for Freedom, Integration, God, Honor, Today.

19. Finks, *The Radical Vision*, 163.

20. Alinsky, *Rules for Radicals*, 68–69.

21. Boyte, *Community Is Possible*, 131.

Chapter Ten

1. Author's interview with Sister Maribeth Larkin, 12 February 1986, San Antonio.

2. Edward T. Chambers, *Organizing for Family and Congregation* (Huntington, New York: Industrial Areas Foundation, 1978), 6.

3. Ibid., 12.

4. Boyte, *Community Is Possible*, 35.

5. "Mediating institutions" is a term used by Peter Berger and Richard John Neuhaus in their book *To Empower People, The Role of Mediating Structures in Public Policy* (Washington, D.C.: American Enterprise Institute for Public Policy, 1971). The concept refers to those institutions standing between the individual in his or her private life and the larger institutions of public life.

Berger and Neuhaus believe that mediating institutions are essential for a vital democratic society and that public policy should not only protect and foster mediating structures but should use them for the realization of social purpose. Cortes and other leaders of the Industrial Areas Foundation believe that their organizations fulfill an essential role in democratic self-government because they serve as mediating institutions.

6. During this period, Cortes also began reading the growing collection of writings by feminist authors such as Betty Friedan, Germaine Greer, Kate Millett, and others.

7. Joe Holley, "What's Going on at City Hall?" *San Antonio Light*, 20 March 1985, n. pag.

Chapter Eleven

1. Father Rodriguez left San Antonio in the mid-1970s and is now a Provencial in the Society of Jesus in New Orleans.

2. Rick Casey, "Church Plays Major Role in Community Group Forging Progress in San Antonio," *National Catholic Reporter*, 12 March 1976, n. pag.

3. Boyte, *Community Is Possible*, 235.

4. Paul Burka, "Second Battle of the Alamo," *Texas Monthly Magazine*, December 1977, 221.

5. Ibid., 222.

6. Jan Jarboe, "Building a Movement," *Civil Rights Digest*, Spring 1977, 43.

7. Burka, "Second Battle," 222.

8. Ibid.

9. Jarboe, "Building a Movement," 44.

10. Tape recording of San Antonio City Council session, 20 August 1974; files of Communities Organized for Public Service, San Antonio.

11. Burka, "Second Battle," 224.

12. Boyte, *Community Is Possible*, 139.

13. Cortes, "Organizing the Community," 13.

14. Burka, "Second Battle," 225.

15. Boyte, *Community Is Possible*, 139–40.

16. Father Albert Benavides was "absolutely essential" to the success of COPS during its first four years, according to Ernie Cortes. Benavides was a strong, charismatic leader who spent most of his ministerial career in a low-income, West Side parish. Growing up in public housing on the West Side, Benavides developed a thirst for knowledge and became an intellectual who brought passion to issues and ideas. He also drew people into his causes. Cortes credits Benavides with introducing him to the works of key biblical scholars and helping him arrive at a "theology" for the kinds of organizing he wanted to do. Benavides drowned while swimming in the Gulf of Mexico in 1984.

17. When Henry Cisneros decided not to run for reelection in 1989, the San Antonio business community supported former Mayor Cockrell, and she

was reelected with only token opposition in 1989. COPS remained neutral in the election.

18. Jarboe, "Building a Movement," 45.

19. Ibid., 46.

20. "COPS Uproar Is Deplored," *San Antonio Light,* 4 February 1977, n. pag.

21. Geoffrey Rips, "New Democratic Models," *Texas Observer,* 9 December 1983, 10.

22. Jarboe, "COPS Eighth Anniversary," n. pag.

23. "Three Years for COPS," *San Antonio News,* 16 November 1976, n. pag.

24. *Today's Catholic,* the newspaper of the archdiocese of San Antonio, 12 August 1977, n. pag.

25. Roddy Stinson writes a regular column for the *San Antonio Express-News.* This quotation is from an undated clipping from the files of Communities Organized for Public Service, San Antonio.

26. City of San Antonio Proclamation, reprinted in COPS 10th Anniversary Program, 10 November 1983.

27. "After Seven Years of Accomplishment, COPS Remains Potent Force in City," *San Antonio Light,* 30 October 1980, n. pag.

28. Rossana Salazar, "White Praises COPS, Affirms Education Goals," *San Antonio Express,* 23 November 1983, n. pag.

29. Boyte, *Community Is Possible,* 144.

30. Rodolfo Resendez, "COPS: Vote Bonds Down 'If Not Ours,'" *San Antonio News,* 19 November 1979, n. pag.

31. Author's interview with Sister Maribeth Larkin, 12 February 1986, San Antonio.

32. Boyte, *Community Is Possible,* 155.

33. Quoted in *God and Money,* a film documentary on the Catholic Bishops' Letter on the Economy, produced by John deGraaf and Betty Jean Bullert, distributed by KCRS-TV, Seattle, Washington, 1985.

34. Author's interview with Toni Hernandez and other women active in Industrial Areas Foundation organizations, 15 February 1986, San Antonio.

35. E.D. Yoes Jr., "COPS Proves Effective," *Texas Observer,* 26 November 1976, 7.

36. Letter from Beatrice Gallegos announcing COPS' 5th convention, 19 November 1978, files of Communities Organized for Public Service, San Antonio.

37. Jan Jarboe, "COPS Warns GGL Remnants," *San Antonio Light,* 22 November 1976, n. pag.

38. *Today's Catholic,* 12 August 1977, n. pag.

39. "SA's Brain Power," *San Antonio Express,* 23 November 1980, n. pag.

40. Rips, "New Democratic Models," 11.

41. Ibid., 10.

Chapter Twelve

1. Unless otherwise noted, this and subsequent quotations come from the author's interview with Sister Maribeth Larkin, 12 February 1986, San Antonio.

2. Ernesto Cortes, Jr., Industrial Areas Foundation training session, 11 July 1986, Los Angeles.

3. Quotation by Father John Coleman, S.J., *A Trade Union Perspective of Laborem Exercens*, Thomas R. Donahue (Washington, D.C.: American Federation of Labor and Congress of Industrial Organizations, 1982), 2.

4. Oliver F. Williams, C.S.C., "The Making of a Pastoral Letter," in *Catholic Social Teaching and the U.S. Economy*, ed. John W. Houck and Oliver Williams (Washington, D.C.: University Press of America, 1984), 11.

5. Gregory Baum, *The Priority of Labor, A Commentary on* Laborem Exercens, *Encyclical Letter of Pope John Paul II* (New York: Paulist Press, 1982), 82.

6. Penny Lernoux, *Cry of the People* (Harmondsworth, U.K.: Penguin Books, 1980), 38.

7. Paulo Freire's philosophy is set out in *The Pedagogy of the Oppressed* (New York: The Seabury Press, 1968).

8. Gustavo Gutierrez, *A Theology of Liberation, History, Politics and Salvation* (Maryknoll, New York: Orbis Books, 1973), 15.

9. Ibid., 95.

10. Industrial Areas Foundation training session, 10 July 1986, Los Angeles.

11. From Robert McAfee Brown, *Theology in a New Key: Responding to Liberation Themes*, quoted in A. James Reichley, *Religion in American Public Life* (Washington, D.C.: The Brookings Institutions, 1985), 261.

12. Ibid.

13. Ibid., 207.

14. From Walter Rauschenbusch, *A Theology for the Social Gospel*, quoted in Reichley, 208.

Chapter Thirteen

1. Because of the bad weather, yellow fever, and competition from other land developers, the Congress of the Republic of Texas decided to move the capital to Austin in 1840.

2. Joe Feagin, "Who Built Houston?" *Texas Observer*, 19 August 1988, 12. This article is an excerpt from Feagin's book, *Free Enterprise City: Houston in Political and Economic Perspective* (New York: Rutgers University Press, 1988).

3. Ibid., 15.

4. *The Texas Almanac and State Industrial Guide, 1982–1983* (Dallas: A.H. Belo Corporation, 1981), 216.

5. Joe Feagin calls the "Suite 8F Crowd" the most powerful elite group in Houston's history because of its cohesion and distinctive personalities, as well as its corporate networks and national and internal resources. Although the actual membership fluctuated from the 1930s to the 1960s, the core of the

group in the early days included Jesse H. Jones, Herman and George Brown (in whose suite at the Lamar Hotel the group met), James A. Elkins Sr., Gus Wortham, and James Abercrombie. Jones headed the Reconstruction Finance Corporation during the New Deal, owned the *Houston Chronicle,* and was a developer who built major buildings in Houston, Fort Worth, and New York. Herman and George Brown's ties with Lyndon Johnson and the growth of their construction firm, Brown and Root, on the basis of government contracts have been well-documented. Elkins was one of the founders of the Vinson and Elkins law firm and headed Houston's largest bank at the time, First City. Elkins also had a major interest in the South's largest insurance firm, American General Insurance Company. Gus Wortham was the founder of American General Insurance and helped build Houston's cultural institutions, supporting local colleges and art facilities. James Abercrombie was an oil entrepreneur who started the Cameron Iron Works, which became one of the world's leading oil tool manufacturing firms, with plants in Europe and Asia, as well as Houston. One of the few women who was welcome in the Suite 8F crowd was Oveta Culp Hobby, who owned the *Houston Post* and a major television station. Mrs. Hobby was the wife of a former Texas governor and the mother of a lieutenant governor (see Chapter 14).

6. Jim Simmon and Robert Relow, Jr., "Downturn hitting blacks harder than others," *Houston Post,* 21 June 1987, n. pag.

7. The prime movers within the Metropolitan Ministries who promoted the organizing project were Protestants Cliff Kirkpatrick, the director of the organization, and the Reverend Dick Siciliano, a Presbyterian minister. Also central to the effort was Father Joseph Fiorenza, who in 1985 would become the bishop of the Catholic diocese of Houston-Galveston.

8. Dwight Silverman, "Group Tackles Big Problem in Big City," *San Antonio Light,* 14 November 1983, n. pag.

9. Texas Industrial Areas Foundation network meeting, 15 February 1986, San Antonio.

10. Geoffrey Rips, untitled column, *In These Times,* 18–24 May 1988, n. pag.

11. Author's interview with Michael Jackson and other leaders, 23 May 1987, Austin.

12. Author's interview with Richard Daly, 12 March 1987, Austin.

13. Bishop Markovsky retired in February 1985 and lived in Houston until his death in March 1990.

14. Metropolitan Congregational Alliance meeting, 16 November 1985, San Antonio.

15. Author's interview with Patrician Ozuna, 11 July 1986, Los Angeles.

16. Rips, "New Democratic Models," 10.

Chapter Fourteen

1. Author's interview with Lt. Gov. William P. Hobby, Jr., 10 October 1986, New York.

2. Unpublished text of speech given by Lieutenant Governor Hobby to the convention of the League of United Latin American Citizens (LULAC), 25 June 1987, Corpus Christi.

3. Author's interview with Saralee Tiede, 30 June 1986, Austin.

4. Author's interview with Richard Daly, 12 March 1987, Austin.

5. Author's interview with Robert Rivera and other Industrial Areas Foundation organizers, 24 January 1986, Austin.

6. Industrial Areas Foundation training session, 10 July 1986, Los Angeles.

7. Dwight Silverman, "COPS: The Seeds of Power," *San Antonio Light,* 13 November 1983, n. pag.

8. Letter to Robert Rivera from Bishop Richard Trelease, Jr. of the Episcopal diocese of the Rio Grande, 21 January 1986.

9. Although Mark White defeated Clements in the 1982 election, many political analysts credited his victory to the well-financed Democratic effort put together by Hobby and Senator Lloyd Bentsen, a moderate like Hobby who had also drawn a wealthy Republican opponent. The ticket was helped by energetic new campaigners who swept into office and included Treasurer Ann Richards, Attorney General Jim Mattox, Agriculture Commissioner Jim Hightower, and Land Commissioner Garry Mauro. In 1986, Hobby and the other Democrats faced only token opposition, but Republican Clements mounted a $16 million campaign to win back his office from Democrat Mark White. Hobby won reelection in 1986, along with the other Democratic candidates who had come into office in 1982. In 1988 Hobby announced he would not seek reelection after his term expired in 1990.

10. Robert Heard, "Perot: COPS Reason School Bill Passed," *San Antonio Express-News,* undated clipping in files of Communities Organized for Public Service, San Antonio.

11. Peter Applebome, "Changing Texas Politics at Its Roots," *New York Times,* 22 May 1988, n. pag.

12. Mayor Cisneros' remarks were passed on to Ernie Cortes by an individual who was present at the meeting.

13. Steve Reed, "Austin Interfaith Quietly Taking Root in Politics," *Austin American,* 9 December 1986, n. pag.

14. Undated flyer paid for by "Employees and Shareholders of Houston Lighting and Power," files of The Metropolitan Organization, Houston.

15. Hobby, LULAC speech.

Chapter Fifteen

1. Texas Industrial Areas Foundation Network meeting, 15 February 1986, San Antonio.

2. Industrial Areas Foundation organizers operating in Texas in 1990 were Gary McNeil and Dana Loy, Austin Interfaith; Perry Perkins and Mattie Crumpton, Allied Communities of Tarrant (ACT); Tom Holler and Mari Brennan, COPS; Pearl Ceasar, The Metro Alliance; Maribeth Larkin, EPISO; Mignonne Konecny, Fort Bend County Interfaith Council; Robert Rivera, Joseph Higgs, and Elizabeth Valdez, TMO; Christine Stephens, Consuelo Tovar, and Tim McCluskey, Valley Interfaith; Rosemary Agneessens, The Border Project; Odilia Korenek, Gulf Coast Organizing Project; Tony Mansueto, Dallas Commission on Justice and Peace; and Steve Jacobs, Texas Industrial Areas Foundation.

3. Author's interview with Nehemiah Davis and other leaders, 23 May 1987, Austin.

4. Author's interview with Sister Maribeth Larkin, 12 February 1986, San Antonio.

5. Boyte, *Community Is Possible*, 147.

6. Casey, "Church Plays Major Role," n. pag.

7. Ibid.

8. The "world as it is" versus the "world as it should be" is an important concept stressed in Industrial Areas Foundation training programs. One of the major IAF critiques of most citizen-based organizations is that they fail to understand the dynamic of change and the reality of power in the "real" world. The IAF tries to teach practical skills to be effective in the world as it is, while maintaining a vision of the world as they feel it should be.

9. The Industrial Areas Foundation is managed by its national director, Edward T. Chambers, and a cabinet of senior organizers: Ernesto Cortes, Jr., Michael Gecan, Arnie Graf, and Larry McNeil. The Board of Directors, which meets annually, includes Archbishop Patrick Flores, Rev. Claude Black, Bishop John Adams A.M.E., Monsignor John Egan, Barry Menuez, and Marvin Wirth.

10. "Wrong Place for Nehemiah," *New York Times*, 31 December 1988, n. pag.

Chapter Sixteen

1. Author's interview with Robert Rivera and other organizers, 24 January 1986, Austin.

2. In 1989, the Industrial Areas Foundation broke with past practice and accepted a planning grant from the Rockefeller Foundation. The purpose of the grant was to develop a model for organizing low-income parents around public education issues. Major goals of the project were to generate more parental involvement in the education of young children and to see if the IAF style of one-on-one organizing could build a constituency-based organization, which could then be integrated into the IAF structure of church-based local organizations.

3. Cortes, "Organizing the Community," 13.

4. All participants in the Industrial Areas Foundation national training programs are given a reprint of a 1933 article by John Herman Randall, Jr. titled "The Importance of Being Unprincipled" (*The American Scholar*, Vol. VII, No. 2, Spring 1933, n. pag.). The thesis is that because politics is nothing but the "practical application of the method of compromise," only two kinds of people can afford the luxury of always acting on principle: those who never act at all because they live in a social vacuum and never try to get anyone else to act, and those who have so much power that they can get what they want simply by issuing commands. Randall says that college professors and Supreme Court justices can afford to act on principle. But everyone else who wants to be effective in politics has to learn to be "unprincipled" enough to compromise in order to see their principles succeed.

5. Quoted in Boyte, *Community Is Possible*, 141, 142.

6. Ibid., 154–55.

7. Cortes, "Organizing the Community," 16.

Epilogue

1. Bernard Crick, *In Defense of Politics* (Harmondsworth, U.K.: Penguin Books, 1980), 21.

2. Ibid., 162.

3. Chambers, "Organizing for Family and Congregation," 3.

4. For a psychological analysis of "meaning," see Viktor E. Frankl, *Man's Search for Meaning* (New York: Simon & Schuster, 1984).

5. Crick, *In Defense*, 23.

6. Quoted in the film documentary *God and Money*.

Index

Hightower, Jim, 5, 209*n*.9
Hispanic people: in El Paso, 162; in
  Houston, 145, 148; organizing,
  176; in San Antonio, 68, 76, 77,
  109, 116; in Texas, 75, 172–173.
  See also West Side (of San
  Antonio)
HL&P. *See* Houston Lighting and
  Power
Hobby, Oveta Culp, 160, 208*n*.5
Hobby, William P., Jr., 55, 157–158,
  161, 168, 209*n*.9; in El Paso, 162,
  164–165; relationship with
  Cortes, 158, 159–160, 165, 169
Holler, Tom, 209*n*.2
Holy Family Catholic Church, 108,
  112–113
Holy spirit, 50, 54
*Honor, Power, Riches, Fame and the
  Love of Women*, 197
Hoover, J. Edgar, 45
Houston, 25–26, 56, 57, 160, 167,
  176, 179, 184; blacks in, 145, 148,
  173; city government of,
  144–145; Cortes organizing in,
  144, 146, 147–150, 152–153, 154;
  development in, 150–151; history
  of, 143–144; poverty in, 145;
  problems organizing in, 145–150.
  See also The Metropolitan
  Organization
Houston-Galveston Diocese, 57, 46,
  149, 208*n*.7
Houston Lighting and Power
  (HL&P), 167–168, 169
Houston Post, 160
Hull House, 82

IAF. *See* Industrial Areas
  Foundation
Immaculate Heart of Mary parish,
  41, 174, 185
"The Importance of Being
  Unprincipled" (John Herman
  Randall Jr.), 210*n*.4
Industrial Areas Foundation (IAF):
  approach to organizing, 59–64,
  194; and *communidades de base*,

141–142; defeats of in Texas,
  168; described by Henry
  Cisneros, 82; on the East Coast,
  180; education issues and, 181,
  210*n*.2; effect on individuals, 21,
  62–63, 196; emphasis on
  relationships, 59–61, 99–100,
  185–186, 194–195; financial and
  structural organziation, 177–180,
  181–182, 210*n*.9; and
  fundraising, 179–180; housing
  issues and, 180–181; influence
  on churches, 154; influence on
  Texas politics, 1–2, 8–9, 24–26,
  125, 165–166, 168–169,
  172–173, 196; institutional base
  of, 139, 174, 177; membership
  base of, 2, 180; opposition to in
  Texas, 163, 166, 168, 173, 184;
  original purpose of, 83; pattern
  for organizing, 86; philosophy of
  organizing, 95–101, 130;
  pluralism of and diversity within,
  152–154, 171–172, 175, 177;
  Protestant involvement in,
  152–153; in Rochester, 89–90;
  role of sponsoring committees,
  178–179; Saul Alinsky begins, 83;
  in Texas, 8, 13, 22, 24, 56, 125,
  153–154, 160, 171–172, 174, 175,
  177, 182, 184–185, 188, 209*n*.2;
  theology and, 93–94, 98–99;
  Training Institute, 91, 95, 129;
  training, 47–54, 99, 176–177,
  203*n*.1, 210*n*.8, 210*n*.4. *See also
  individual IAF organizations*
Inman, Bobby Ray, 43
Institute for Juvenile Research, 82
Interfaith Network. *See* Texas
  Interfaith Network
Iron Rule, 15, 50, 63, 106, 115,
  129, 150, 174, 179, 185

Jackson, Michael, 149
Jacobs, Steve, 209*n*.2
Jefferson, Thomas, 24, 83, 84, 141
Jesus and the Zealots, 131
John Paul II, Pope, 122, 135, 138